Name: ______________________________

Class: ______________________________

Teacher: ______________________________

Islamic Studies Textbook Level 6

Minhaj-ul-Quran International

Published by

Minhaj-ul-Quran Publications
30 Brindley Road
Manchester
M16 9HQ (UK)

Acknowledgements

Bilal Hussain, Safina Nazir, Muhammad Zeeshan Qadri, Ali Akbar, Raffiq Patel and M. Dawood Mehmood

A sincere thank you to Ajmal Khan for his assistance in the design work

ISBN: 978-1-908229-60-1

www.minhajpublications.com

www.islamforkids.org.uk

First published August 2018

Printed by Mega Printing in Turkey

Islamic Studies
Textbook Level 6

Series Editors

Waqas Ahmed Amin

Jawed Iqbal Tahiri

Mariam Khalid

Series Director

Tahseen Khalid

Minhaj-ul-Quran International

Preface

In the name of Allah, the Most Merciful, the Most Kind.

WE PRAISE ALLAH that the Muslim community has come a long way since the days when the first immigrants settled in Britain. From that time till today, there have been significant developments in the quality of educational material being produced by British Muslims. Many advancements have been made in this regard such that English is fast becoming one of the academic languages of Islam, alongside Arabic, Persian, Urdu and Turkish.

The importance of education cannot be overstated. The British Muslim community has put great effort into imparting Islamic knowledge to their children. Islamic classes and religious seminaries have been established up and down the country for the single goal of teaching the coming generations the fundamentals of their religion. Among those that have been at the forefront in this regard is Minhaj-ul-Quran International, a global organisation with branches in over 90 countries.

As an organisation, Minhaj-ul-Quran International seeks to uplift Muslims worldwide through the revival of education and spirituality. It established its first branch in the United Kingdom in the late 1980s and founded its first centre in the 1990s. For more than two decades it has endeavoured to provide for the educational and spiritual needs of the Muslim diaspora of Great Britain.

The 'Islam for Kids' initiative is part of the longstanding services of Minhaj-ul-Quran International. This Islamic Studies series was produced and developed by second and third generation British scholars, who are trained classically in the traditional Islamic sciences, alongside QTS (Qualified Teaching Status) accredited teachers. It is an indigenous and local endeavour by the UK branch of Minhaj-ul-Quran International to fulfil the educational needs of native English-speaking students.

The Syllabus

The 'Islam for Kids' Islamic Studies series has been split into six levels with each level corresponding to the years of the state-funded education system in the UK. It is recommended to start level one at the age of 5 when the child starts year one at primary school and to complete level 6 by the age of 11 when the child completes his or her primary school education. However, the series can be started earlier at an earlier age or later depending on the ability of the student.

The six levels have been grouped into three stages, with each stage consisting of two levels. In the first stage, which consists of levels one and two, the aim is to ease the child into understanding Islamic concepts and terminology. The purpose of this stage is not to burden the child with technical knowledge about Islam, but rather to simply instil in them a sense of Muslim identity and to explore key Islamic concepts.

Traditionally, Muslim parents have been advised to have a play-based approach with their children's learning for the first seven years and then to formally teach them for the next seven years. Following this advice, in the first two years of the syllabus, a more visual approach has been adopted with the text being kept at a minimum. This enables the content to be taught in a child-friendly manner and allows teachers and parents to make the lessons more interactive and engaging for the child.

The second stage of the syllabus begins at level three when the child reaches seven years of age. From this level onwards, a more formal approach to learning is adopted. Many of the concepts in the first stage are revisited, but instead of being largely pictorial, they are more text-based so that the key concepts can be conveyed in detail to the child and to encourage the child to start thinking about the content in more depth.

In the third stage of the syllabus, which consists of levels five and six, the series shifts to a more text-heavy approach. This is to encourage the child to learn independently and practice their key reading and comprehension skills. The content at this level increases in difficulty to engage students academically and to raise the standard of literacy and understanding of Islamic concepts.

The concepts from the previous two stages are revisited in this third stage but in much more detail. Parents and teachers alike will find this stage beneficial as reading material to help prepare in terms of subject knowledge for teaching the lessons in the earlier two stages. In this way, the three stages work together to ease the child into becoming well acquainted with Islamic terminology, concepts and values.

By the end of this syllabus, the child will have acquired the essential Islamic knowledge (*Fard `Ayn*) for them to be able to live their life as a practising Muslim. This Islamic Studies series is an excellent resource for parents to lay the foundation for their child's learning. If Allah wills, further levels will be added to this syllabus, thus enhancing the child's understanding of Islam and enabling them to become lifelong learners of the Islamic tradition.

The First Edition

In preparation of this series, authentic and reliable content was taken from the works of great scholars who represent Islamic orthodoxy. Some of the books that were consulted in the creation of the content were:

- Imam ash-Shurunbulali's *Nur al-Idah* and its commentary, *Maraqi al-Falah*
- Imam al-Laqqani's *Jawharah at-Tawhid*
- Shaykh Salih Farfur's *ar-Risalah an-Nafi`ah fi `Ilm at-Tawhid*
- Imam Ibn Hisham's *as-Sirah an-Nabawiyyah* (including its English rendition by Martin Lings)
- Imam Ibn Kathir's *al-Bidayah wa an-Nihayah*
- and the many hadith collections compiled by the founder of Minhaj-ul-Quran, Shaykh-ul-Islam Dr Muhammad Tahir-ul-Qadri

The contents of these books have been adapted for children at an age appropriate level while keeping in consideration the specific needs and requirements of Western Muslims.

We are eager to hear from the wider community and to gain feedback regarding the series. For this purpose, we have set up an email address for you to send us your feedback. You can contact us at the following address: **feedback@fmriuk.org**.

Acknowledgements

Before closing, I would like to thank my co-editors, Jawed Iqbal Tahiri and Mariam Khalid, for their commitment and assistance in helping to prepare and develop the contents of this syllabus. I would also like to thank the Series Director, Tahseen Khalid, for his great determination and support in bringing this series to fruition.

I would also like to thank Bilal Hussain for his assistance in preparing the outline of the syllabus and the Textbook Review Team (Safina Nazir, Muhammad Zeeshan Qadri, Ali Akbar, Raffiq Patel and Dawood Mehmood) for their feedback and support. A special thank you goes to Ajmal Khan for the outstanding devotion he has shown in improving and further developing the design work.

I pray to Allah that He accepts our efforts and makes it a means of salvation for us in this life and the next, and we pray that this series becomes a means of uplifting the Ummah for generations to come.

Amin bi-jahi Sayyid al-Mursalin ﷺ.

Waqas Ahmed Amin
Minhaj-ul-Quran Publications
1st Dhu al-Hijjah 1439 AH/12th August 2018 CE

Contents

Lesson 1

Belief in Allah – Attributes

Attributes are the qualities or characteristics of a person or thing. Human beings have attributes, and they can be either good or bad. Some examples of good attributes are loyalty, intelligence and fairness; and some examples of bad ones are hatred, weakness and laziness.

The Attributes of Allah

Allah has attributes, but Allah's attributes are not like human ones. All of Allah's attributes are good, and there are no faults or weakness in any of them. The following five attributes of Allah are necessary for every Muslim to believe in:

1. No Beginning

Allah does not have a beginning. There was never a time when Allah did not exist. Nothing came before Allah, and it is not the case that Allah did not exist and then came into existence, because Allah always existed.

From the Beautiful Names of Allah that show this meaning is the name: '**al-Awwal**' (The First).

2. No End

Allah does not have an end. There will never be a time when Allah will not exist because Allah will always continue to exist. Allah will never die or come to an end.

From the Beautiful Names of Allah that show this meaning are the names: '**al-Akhir**' (The Last) and '**al-Baqi**' (The Eternal).

3. Not Like His Creation

Allah is not like anyone or anything else. There is nothing in the whole universe that is similar or like Allah. Whatever image or thought comes to our mind is not like Allah, because Allah is transcendent, i.e. He is beyond our minds and cannot be imagined by us.

From the Beautiful Names of Allah that show this meaning is the name: '**al-Quddus**' (The Holy).

4. Self-Sufficient

Allah is self-sufficient. He is absolute and independent. Allah does not need anyone or anything, and He does not need any help or assistance. We all, however, need Allah and depend on Him because He is the One Who makes and controls everything.

From the Beautiful Names of Allah that show this meaning are the names: '**al-Malik**' (The King), '**al-Qayyum**' (The Subsisting) and '**as-Samad**' (The Absolute).

5. Oneness

Allah is One in His being, attributes and actions. He does not have any partner in His being or an equal in His attributes. He is not made up of parts and cannot be made smaller or bigger. His oneness means He is unique.

From the Beautiful Names of Allah that show this meaning is the name: '**al-Wahid**' (The One).

Note: All of Allah's attributes, whether they are related to His being or actions, have these five characteristics.

The Attributes of Allah's Being

Some of Allah's attributes belong to His being and others belong to His actions. The following attributes belong to Allah's being and it is obligatory on every Muslim to believe in them. They are:

1. Life

Allah is Ever-Living. His life has no beginning and no end, and it is not like our life, because we are dependent on Allah for our life, but Allah is not dependent on anyone or anything for His life.

From the Beautiful Names of Allah that show this meaning is the name: '**al-Hayy**' (The Living).

2. Knowledge

Allah knows everything. Nothing is hidden from Allah and there is never a moment when Allah does not have perfect knowledge about everything. Unlike our knowledge, Allah's knowledge does not increase or decrease. We learn things gradually after not knowing, but Allah has always had perfect knowledge about everything.

From the Beautiful Names of Allah which show this meaning are the names: '**al-`Alim**' (The All-Knowing) and '**al-Khabir**' (The All-Aware).

3. Will

Everything takes place by the will of Allah. No one can force Allah to do anything. It is Allah Who decides everything. No one can do anything unless Allah permits it. Once Allah decides something, it takes place, and no one can stop it from happening.

From the Beautiful Names of Allah that show this meaning is the name: '**Malik al-Mulk**' (The Master of the Kingdom).

4. Power

Allah is the All-Powerful. He has power over everything. Allah does not need anyone's help, but we all need Allah's help because it is only Allah who has real power. Our power is not like Allah's, because our power is dependent on Allah and Allah's power is not dependant on anyone or anything.

From the Beautiful Names of Allah that show this meaning are the names: '**al-Qadir**' (The Powerful), '**al-Muqtadir**' (The Greatly Powerful), '**al-Qawi**' (The Most Powerful) and '**al-Matin**' (The Very Powerful).

5. Sight

Allah is the All-Seeing. He sees everything. Nothing is hidden from Him. Allah does not need anything to see. His sight is perfect and unique.

From the Beautiful Names of Allah that show this meaning is the name: '**al-Basir**' (The All-Seeing).

6. Hearing

Allah is the All-Hearing. He hears everything. Allah hears everything that we say. There are no limits to His hearing because He can hear every sound.

From the Beautiful Names of Allah that show this meaning is the name: '**as-Sami`**' (The All-Hearing).

7. Speech

Allah has the attribute of speech. This means Allah speaks, however, His speech is not like our speech. When we speak, we make sounds and we use words, but Allah's speech is not like this as His speech is timeless and eternal like all His attributes.

Allah is Ever-Living, All-Knowing, Willing, All-Powerful, All-Seeing, All-Hearing and Speaking.

Note: We use the same words when we talk about Allah's attributes of being and action because that is the only way we can understand, but the words do not mean the same thing. For example, Allah's attribute of power has the five characteristics of not having a beginning or end, not being like His creation, being self-sufficient and one, whereas the human attribute of power has the opposite of these five characteristics, i.e. it has a beginning and end, similar to other created beings, not self-sufficient but dependent on Allah's power, and divisible. Thus, the word may be the same, but its meaning is different.

The Attributes of Allah's Actions

Allah has many actions. They all are His act of creation. His act of creation is eternal and endless, and it is a display of His great power.

Among His acts of creation are:

- Creating something from nothing
- Creating without a former example
- Creating different forms and shapes
- Creating food and sustenance
- Creating life
- Causing death
- Bringing back to life

In general, we believe that all of Allah's attributes are good. None of His attributes are imperfect. Allah does not have any bad characteristics, such as lying, not fulfilling promises or treating others unfairly.

Lesson 2

The Grades of the Halal and Haram

Allah is the Most-Wise. He gave us laws to follow so that we can live a virtuous (good) life. Following these laws is for our own benefit. When we obey Allah's laws, we get the best of this life and the life hereafter.

The laws of Allah are found in the Qur'an and the Sunnah. The Qur'an is the last and final revelation sent to the last and final Prophet, our master Muhammad ﷺ. The Sunnah is the way of the Prophet ﷺ. It is how he lived his life and it is the practical example and explanation of the Qur'an. By studying the Qur'an and the Sunnah, we know what things are allowed for us and what things are not.

Halal (lawful) and Haram (unlawful) are not just to do with the things that we eat and drink. They cover every aspect of life and the things that we do in our everyday lives. Halal and Haram are the limits that tell us what we can and cannot do. If we love Allah, we should always stay within the limits and not break them.

Even though Halal and Haram are broad terms that relate to every aspect of our life, not everything is simply Halal or Haram. There are also different grades of the Halal and Haram, which we must also know about. There are 11 grades in total. However, we will discuss some of them here in a simplified manner.

The Grades of the Halal

Halal (lawful) is a general term that refers to the things Muslims are allowed to do. At a basic level it has three grades:

1. OBLIGATORY

This is something that we MUST do because Allah

and His Prophet Muhammad ﷺ command us to do it. We use the Arabic terms '**Fard**' and '**Wajib**' for things that are obligatory. (**Note:** Within the obligatory grade, Fard is higher than Wajib.)

From the grades of the Halal, the obligatory is the highest grade and examples of it are: praying five times a day, fasting in the month of Ramadan, performing the Hajj once in a lifetime, respecting one's parents and teachers, keeping one's body and clothes clean, seeking necessary Islamic knowledge, fulfilling the rights of others and treating people fairly.

2. RECOMMENDED

This is something we SHOULD do because Allah and His Prophet Muhammad ﷺ want us to do it. We use the Arabic terms '**Sunnah**' and '**Mustahabb**' for things that are recommended.

From the grades of the Halal, this is the next level down and some examples of it are: performing extra prayers with the five daily prayers, staying in Wudu' all day, reciting the Qur'an every day, going to gatherings of Dhikr and Salat `ala al-Nabi ﷺ, giving gifts to friends and family and feeding them, looking after your home and school, helping your teacher, reading a book to increase your knowledge and even wearing a seatbelt when travelling in a car.

3. PERMISSIBLE

This is something we CAN do because Allah and His Prophet Muhammad ﷺ have NOT stopped us from doing it. We use the Arabic term '**Mubah**' for things that are permissible.

From the grades of the Halal, this is the lowest level and it is the largest because it includes many things that we do in our lives. Some examples of it are: eating chocolates, crisps and ice cream, drinking fizzy drinks, playing with toys, drawing or colouring, watching cartoons or films, holding a party for your friends, playing or watching sports or riding a bike.

In Summary

We MUST do the things that are obligatory (i.e. Fard and Wajib). Allah has not given us any choice. If we leave the obligatory actions on purpose or fail to practice them, then it is a major sin. The person who misses these actions on purpose or fails to practice them must ask Allah for forgiveness and try to make up for it.

We SHOULD do the things that are recommended (i.e. Sunnah and Mustahabb). However, there is no sin in not doing them, but reward will be given to the person who does practice them.

Note: There are some Sunnah, such as the Sunnah Mu`akkadah, that are close to the obligatory in their importance. We should NOT miss them out unless we have a valid excuse. Making a habit of missing them is a sin.

We CAN do the things that are permissible (Mubah). It is our choice if we want to do them or not. However, even though we are allowed to do them and it is not a sin, there is no reward in doing them.

The Grades of the Halal

The Grades of Haram

Haram (unlawful) is a general term that refers to the things Muslims are NOT allowed to do. At a basic level it has two grades:

1. IMPERMISSIBLE

This is something that we MUST NOT do because Allah and His Prophet Muhammad ﷺ have stopped us from doing it. We use the Arabic term '**Haram**' for things that are impermissible.

This is the higher of the two grades and examples of it are: stealing, lying, backbiting, swearing, hitting others, eating pork, drinking wine, missing the five daily prayers or the fast in Ramadan, disobeying parents and being rude and disrespectful to one's teachers and elders.

2. DISLIKED

This is something we SHOULD NOT do because Allah and His Prophet Muhammad ﷺ do not want us to do it. We use the Arabic term '**Makruh**' for things that are disliked.

This is the lower grade and some examples of it are: wasting water when doing Wudu', rushing the prayer, wasting time and money, leaving the lights on without a need, not finishing your food, not doing your homework, not looking after your health, doing something dangerous to yourself or to others and not asking permission when borrowing something.

In Summary

We MUST NOT do the things that are impermissible (Haram). Allah has not given us any choice in this matter. If we do something impermissible, we must ask Allah for forgiveness straightway because it is a major sin. If Allah does not forgive us for this sin, then He will punish us in the Hellfire. So we must never do something Haram in the first place.

We SHOULD NOT do the things that are disliked (Makruh) because doing them is a minor sin and something that Allah does not like. If we do them often, then they become major sins. So, we should try our best to avoid them as much as possible and ask Allah for forgiveness when we do any of the disliked (Makruh) actions.

The Grades of the Haram

The Halal and Haram Scale

Like day and night, Halal and Haram are opposites. The Halal (lawful) includes the obligatory (Fard and Wajib), recommended (Sunnah and Mustahabb) and the permissible (Mubah); while the Haram (unlawful) includes the impermissible (Haram) and the disliked (Makruh).

The following scale shows the relationship between Halal and Haram.

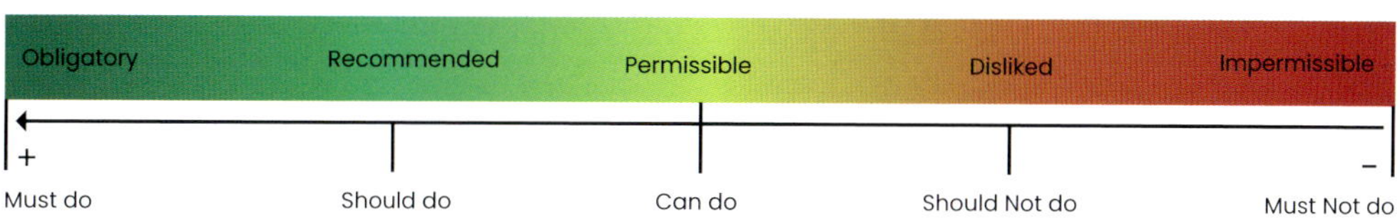

From this scale, we can see that the obligatory (Fard and Wajib) is the opposite of the impermissible (Haram), while recommended (Sunnah and Mustahabb) is the opposite of disliked (Makruh). Permissible (Mubah) is in the middle and it is a neutral grade in between the two opposite sides.

How does Something Become Haram?

Something becomes Haram (unlawful and impermissible) for us when Allah and His Prophet Muhammad ﷺ tell us in the Qur'an and the Sunnah that it is unlawful (Haram).

Saying that something is Haram when Allah and His Prophet Muhammad ﷺ did not forbid us from it is a major sin because it is no less than lying about Allah and His Prophet ﷺ (an-Nahl 16: People who do this cause arguments between Muslims and break the unity of the Muslim Ummah.

All the Haram things have been mentioned clearly in the Qur'an and nothing has been left out. The Qur'an has listed the things that are Haram and it does not list the things that are Halal.

If the Qur'an does not say that something is Haram, then it means that it is permissible (Mubah), because there are more permissible (Mubah) actions than impermissible (Haram) ones. If something was Haram (unlawful) it would have been listed in the Qur'an in the first place.

If a person wants to know whether something is Haram, they should first see if Allah and His Prophet ﷺ have made it Haram. If he or she finds that the Qur'an does not say that it is Haram, then it means it is permissible (Mubah) and when something is permissible (Mubah), it means it is Halal (lawful) because it is inside the limit set by Allah.

Lesson 3

Sirah: The Treaty of Hudaybiyah

The Quraysh and the other tribes that worked with them during the Battle of Khandaq were in great shock that the Muslims defeated them. An army as great as theirs had never been defeated by a small number of people before. The Quraysh were still angry about losing the battle even a year later.

The Trip to Makkah

Towards the end of the 6th year after the Hijrah (migration from Makkah to Madinah), the Prophet ﷺ announced that he will be travelling to Makkah to perform the `Umrah (the Minor Pilgrimage). The Companions were very excited when they heard this and around 1400 of them set off for Makkah to do the `Umrah with the Prophet ﷺ.

On this special journey, the Prophet ﷺ and the Companions wore the Ihram and took with them the animals to sacrifice after the pilgrimage. They did not take any of their weapons, except for their swords and hunting equipment which in those days was normal for the Arabs when they travelled. Many women also went on this journey to Makkah standing side by side with their men. This showed the Quraysh that the Muslims came in peace. It was clear from the behaviour of the Muslims that they only planned to visit the Ka`bah and to perform the `Umrah; they did not want to start a war against anyone.

The Quraysh React

When the Quraysh found out that the Muslims were coming to Makkah, they quickly gathered a meeting of their leaders to discuss what to do with them. They did not want to let them enter Makkah, knowing that a year earlier they themselves were unable to enter Madinah with their large army. If the Muslims walked right into Makkah, it would embarrass them in front of all the other Arabs and it would show them that they were weak. So, they were determined to stop the Muslims from coming to Makkah.

The Quraysh stopped the Muslims outside Makkah in a place called Hudaybiyah. They sent a man called `Urwah bin Mas`ud to speak to the Muslims to find a solution to the situation. They needed to find a way to send the Muslims back without looking like they stopped the pilgrims from visiting the Ka`bah. When Prophet Muhammad ﷺ let `Urwah bin Mas`ud meet with him, he told him that they only planned to visit the Ka`bah and to perform the `Umrah, and that they had no intention of fighting with them.

The Companions' Love and Respect for the Prophet ﷺ

`Urwa returned to the Quraysh and delivered the Prophet's message. While he was with the Prophet ﷺ, he noticed the way the Companions behaved around their Prophet. When he returned to Makkah, he told the Quraysh of his amazement, saying, "O Quraysh! By Allah, I have been to the kings and to Caesar, Khosrau and Najashi, yet I have never seen any of them respected by their followers as much as Muhammad is respected by his Companions. By Allah, if he spat, the spit would fall in the hand of one of them who would rub it on his face and skin. If he ordered them to do something, they would carry out his order immediately. If he performed ablution, they would struggle with each other to take the water that was left over; and when they spoke, they would lower their voices and would not look at his face constantly out of respect for him." (al-Bukhari)

The Companions' immense love and respect for the Holy Prophet ﷺ had a great impact on `Urwah bin Mas`ud. He told the Quraysh about this so that they would know how important of a leader the Prophet ﷺ was.

The Prophet's Miracle

While the Muslims were staying in Hudaybiyah, they did not have much water and there were no water wells around. They felt thirsty and needed water to drink. There was a small bottle of water lying in front of the Prophet ﷺ and he performed the ablution. When he did this, the people rushed towards him, so he asked them, "What is the matter with you?" The Companions replied, "O Messenger of Allah, we have no water to perform ablution, or to drink, except what is lying with you." When the Prophet ﷺ heard this, he put his hand into the bottle and water began to gush out between his fingers like fountains. The Companions drank the water till they were full, and they also performed the ablution (al-Bukhari).

The Promise of Loyalty to Prophet Muhammad ﷺ

The Prophet ﷺ sent one of the Companions to the Quraysh to continue talks with them to come to a solution. However, when the Companion reached them, some people of the Quraysh got angry and killed the camel that he was riding. Other people stopped them and saved the Companion's life and sent him back. The Prophet ﷺ was saddened by this, so he sent his son-in-law `Uthman bin `Affan to talk to the Quraysh because `Uthman had a good relationship with many of his relatives who were from the Quraysh.

When `Uthman met the Quraysh, they welcomed him warmly. He gave them the Prophet's message that they only want to perform the `Umrah and have not come to fight. After delivering the Prophet's message, the Quraysh gave `Uthman a chance to perform the Tawaf around the Ka`bah. However, `Uthman refused, saying, "I will not perform the Tawaf until the Prophet ﷺ performs it first." (al-Bayhaqi) When the Prophet ﷺ found out about this later, he was pleased with `Uthman for his loyalty and his devotion.

Days had passed and `Uthman had not yet returned from the Quraysh. The Muslims were worried because they heard news that he had been killed. They did not know that he was being held by them. The news of his death brought anger to the Muslims. So, the Prophet ﷺ sat under a tree and called the Muslims to give him their pledge of allegiance (a promise to be loyal) that they would remain in Hudaybiyah until they had taken revenge for the murder of `Uthman.

One by one the Companions came to the Prophet ﷺ and they put their hand in the Prophet's hand and pledged their allegiance. This pledge of allegiance is known as 'Bay`at ar-Ridwan' (the Pledge of Contentment) because Allah was pleased with all those Companions who gave their pledge. It is also known as 'Bay`at ash-Shajara' (the Pledge of the Tree), because the Prophet ﷺ was sitting under a tree when the Companions gave their pledge to him. The 1400 Companions who gave the pledge of allegiance on this day have a special status in Islam and Allah praised them in the Qur'an (al-Fath 48:18).

The Quraysh are Ready to Listen

When the news of the pledge reached the Quraysh, they released `Uthman immediately.

This pledge showed them that the Muslims were determined and needed to be taken seriously. So, the Quraysh sent a man called Suhayl bin `Amr, to the Muslims to find a solution. The Prophet ﷺ was pleased to see Suhayl because he knew that the Quraysh now wanted to reach an agreement with them. After a long discussion, an agreement was reached between the two sides and a peace treaty was signed.

This peace treaty is known as 'Sulh al-Hudaybiyah' (the Treaty of Hudaybiyah). In the Treaty of Hudaybiyah it was agreed that there would be ten years of peace between the Muslims and the Quraysh. If someone from the Quraysh came to Madinah the Muslims would have to return him to Makkah, but if someone from the Muslims came to Makkah, the Quraysh did not have to send him back to Madinah. It was also agreed that the Muslims would not perform `Umrah that year. They would have to return home and come back the following year and stay in Makkah for only three days.

The Prophet of Peace and Love ﷺ

When these conditions of the treaty were agreed upon, `Umar bin al-Khattab was upset. He was upset that the Muslims were agreeing to a treaty that was unfair because most of the conditions seemed to help the Quraysh and not the Muslims. He could not understand how the Muslims could accept this agreement when they were on the true path. He could not control his feelings, so he went to the Prophet ﷺ and asked, "O Messenger of Allah, are you not the Messenger of Allah?" And the Prophet ﷺ replied, "Yes." "Are we not Muslims?" `Umar asked. The Prophet ﷺ replied, "Yes." "Are they not idol worshippers?" asked `Umar. "Yes," the Prophet replied, and then he said, "one day we will enter Makkah and perform the `Umrah; it does not have to be this year." After hearing this, `Umar became calm and remained silent in front of the Prophet ﷺ and asked him for forgiveness.

The Prophet ﷺ called `Ali bin Abi Talib to write down the conditions of the treaty. `Ali began writing with the words, 'In the name of Allah', but Suhayl bin `Amr complained about this, saying, "We do not recognise this. Write: 'In your name, O God'."

The Prophet ﷺ accepted and he told `Ali to write that instead. Then `Ali continued by writing, 'This is a peace treaty between Muhammad, the Messenger of Allah, and Suhayl bin `Amr'. Again, Suhayl complained about this, saying, "If we believed that you were the Messenger of Allah, we would not have fought with you. Instead, write your name and your father's name."

The Prophet ﷺ accepted this and ordered `Ali to write that instead, but `Ali could not bring himself to do it. He could not cross out the words, 'Messenger of Allah' after he had written them. So, the Prophet ﷺ took the pen from `Ali and crossed out the words himself. Through his actions, the Prophet ﷺ showed how he was a Prophet of Peace and Love. His example showed that he loved peace and not war, because the Prophet ﷺ always tried to get things done peacefully first to avoid going to war with his enemies.

During the discussions of the peace treaty, the Bakr tribe joined the side of the Quraysh whereas the Khuza`ah tribe joined the Muslims. Both of these tribes had been at war with each other and they agreed to follow the peace treaty and to stop the fighting. The Treaty of Hudaybiyah allowed any Arab tribes to join either side if they followed the peace treaty.

The Prophet ﷺ Fulfils His Promises

Once the treaty had been finalised, Abu Jandal, who was one of the Muslim prisoners taken by the Quraysh, came to the Prophet ﷺ asking to be freed. But Suhayl bin `Amr did not agree to his release saying that the treaty had been finalised and that according to the treaty Abu Jandal must be returned to Makkah. As Abu Jandal was being taken away, he screamed to the top of his voice "O Muslims, how can you leave me to be punished by the idol worshippers?" The Muslims could not control their anger any longer and they begged the Prophet ﷺ to not let him go, but the Prophet ﷺ told Abu Jandal to remain patient, because one day Allah would find a way out for him.

The Great Victory

The Muslims could not do `Umrah that year and had to return to Madinah as part of the agreement of the treaty. So, the Prophet ﷺ commanded the Muslims to sacrifice their camels and for the men to shave their heads so that they could remove their Ihram. The idea of returning to Madinah without performing the `Umrah came as a great shock to the Muslims, and no one moved. The Muslims could not believe that they were giving up in this way, when they knew they were on the true and right path. They were so shocked that they just remained sitting unable to understand what had happened.

Seeing that the Muslims were not moving, the Prophet ﷺ was saddened and he sat in his tent. During this time, Mother of the Believers Umm Salamah suggested to the Prophet ﷺ that he should go out and sacrifice his camel without saying a single word to anyone. When the Prophet ﷺ did this, the Muslims got up because of their obedience and love for the Prophet ﷺ and started sacrificing their camels and shaving their heads to follow the example of the Prophet ﷺ.

Once the Muslims had completed their sacrifice, they made their way back to Madinah. On the way back, the Prophet ﷺ received a revelation from Allah. Allah informed the Prophet ﷺ of a 'Clear Victory' for the Muslims (al-Fath 48:1). He was happy with the Muslims and He informed the Prophet ﷺ that one day they would enter Makkah and perform the `Umrah (al-Fath 48:27). Even though the Muslims did not realise it at the time, within a few years they would receive many great victories from Allah.

Lesson 4

The Ritual Bath (Ghusl)

Keeping clean is extremely important. Prophet Muhammad ﷺ said, *"Cleanliness is half of faith (Iman)."* (Muslim)

We cannot perform the Salah, touch the Qur'an or perform the Tawaf without being in a **state of ritual purity (Taharah)**. Even outside of worship, we should remain pure. If we want to develop spiritually and get closer to Allah, we should remain in a state of ritual purity all the time.

One of the important ways that we can remain clean is to have a bath or shower. In Islam, the ritual bath is known as '**Ghusl**', and there are specific conditions for it to be done properly. We must know the rules of doing Ghusl and what makes it obligatory so that we can worship Allah correctly and stay in a state of ritual purity (Taharah).

When to Perform the Ghusl?

As Muslims, it is extremely important to maintain our personal hygiene. We are rewarded by Allah for doing this and it is also a way of getting closer to Him. People who do not maintain hygiene and always remain dirty are easily affected by Shaytan and they can suffer from mental illness because of it. Therefore, we must remain clean and pure all the time and give importance to our personal hygiene.

It is **obligatory** to have a bath after a wet-dream This is when a white sticky liquid comes out from the private part during sleep. If someone finds such a liquid in the morning, then they need to perform the Ghusl. Doing Wudu' alone is not enough.

Other than having good personal hygiene, there are times when we take a bath or shower as an act of worship. We take a bath or shower on some special occasions to receive reward from Allah and to follow in the footsteps of our beloved Prophet Muhammad ﷺ.

Having a bath on the following occasions is **recommended**:

1. On Friday, for the Jumu`ah prayer.
2. On the two days of Eid, for the `Id prayer.
3. Before putting on the Ihram.
4. On special nights, like Laylat al-Qadr and Laylat al-Bara'ah (15th Night of Sha`ban).
5. When entering Makkah and Madinah.

We should take a bath or shower regularly. Especially when it is a hot day or after playing sports when we sweat a lot, we should take a bath or shower to remove the bad smell from our body.

It is a good habit for children under the age of 11 to take a bath or shower at least once or twice a week, but as you get older, you will need to increase this to 2-3 times a week. Try not to have a bath or shower every day, because it can make your skin dry and leave it without the important oils that it needs.

How to do the Ghusl Properly?

When we perform the Ghusl, we need to make sure that every part of our body is washed with water. If something prevents water from reaching the skin, such as a tight-fitting watch or ring, it needs to be removed first before getting into the bath or shower.

Washing every part of the body is the basic rule of the Ghusl. Not fulfilling this rule means that your Ghusl is incomplete and that you have not attained the state of ritual purity (Taharah). Praying without ritual purity (Taharah) means that the prayer is invalid, and it needs to be repeated.

To perform the Ghusl (ritual bath), do the following:

1. Make an intention in your heart that you will be doing the Ghusl (ritual bath).

2. Recite the Tasmiyah (i.e. Bismillaah) in your heart. (Do not say Allah's name aloud in the bathroom.)

3. Wash both hands up to the wrist.

4. Wash away any dirt on your body.

5. Wash the private parts.

From here you will be making the Wudu'
(the ritual ablution)

6. Rinse the mouth by gargling.
(Make sure the water reaches your throat.)

7. Rinse the nose and clean your nostrils up to the soft part of the nose.

8. Wash the face.

9. Wash the right arm up to and including the elbow, and then the left arm.

10. Wet your hands and wipe them over your head and ears.

11. Wash the right foot up to and including the ankle, and then the left foot.

(This can be delayed to the end if the used water makes a puddle at one's feet.)

Wash the rest of the body making sure every part of it is washed properly and nothing is left dry.

12. Pour water over the head three times. (Make sure the water reaches the scalp.)

13. Pour water over the right shoulder three times and wash under your armpits.

14. Pour water over the left shoulder three times and wash under your armpits.

15. Pour water over the whole body three times and make sure every part of your body is clean.

There are three **obligatory** acts in the Ghusl, and they are: rinsing the mouth by gargling, rinsing the nose and washing the whole body.

It is **recommended** to rub the body and to use soap so that the body is cleaned properly.

Some Important Points

There are some important things to know about the Ghusl (ritual bath). These have been listed below:

- Performing the Ghusl is one of the two ways of achieving Taharah. If a person performs the Ghusl properly, then that person does not need to repeat the Wudu' (ritual ablution). This is because in the Ghusl, you also wash the parts that need to be washed in the Wudu', and so by doing the Ghusl you have also done the Wudu'.

- The above method of doing Ghusl is the Sunnah method (i.e. the way Prophet Muhammad ﷺ used to do Ghusl). However, taking a bath or shower in any way completes the Ghusl so long as the mouth and nose are rinsed properly, and no part of the body is left dry. It is not obligatory to make an intention to perform Ghusl but doing so will increase the reward. The same also applies to the Wudu' (the ritual ablution).

- It is important to make sure that the water reaches every part of the body. If there is something that stops the water from touching the skin, it must be removed first or loosened so the water can get through. Things like nail varnish, makeup and face painting must be removed before performing the Ghusl.

- The Ghusl must be performed in a place where you cannot be seen by anyone. It is obligatory not to reveal one's nakedness (`awrah) to anyone.

- While doing the Wudu', it is recommended to face the Qiblah. However, when performing the Ghusl, do not face the Qiblah because you will be naked. Facing the Qiblah without wearing clothes is a sinful act, just like facing the Qiblah while going on the toilet.

Lesson 5

Tawhid and Shirk

As Muslims, we believe Allah is one and unique, and that He and only He is worthy of worship. The belief of Allah's oneness, as taught to us by Prophet Muhammad ﷺ, is called '**Tawhid**'.

In the Qur'an, Allah describes His tawhid in the following words:

بِسْمِ اللّٰهِ الرَّحْمٰنِ الرَّحِيْمِ

قُلْ هُوَ اللّٰهُ أَحَدٌ. اَللّٰهُ الصَّمَدُ. لَمْ يَلِدْ وَلَمْ يُوْلَدْ

وَلَمْ يَكُن لَّهُ كُفُوًا أَحَدٌ

In the name of Allah, the Most Merciful, the Most Kind.

"(O Prophet!) Declare: 'He is Allah – the One. Allah is the Self-Sufficient and Independent. He did not father anyone, nor was He born. No one is equal to Him.'" (al-Ikhlas 112:1-4)

There are three aspects of tawhid (the oneness of Allah):

1. Oneness of Allah’s **being**
2. Oneness of Allah’s **attributes**
3. Oneness of Allah’s **actions**

We will discuss each one in detail.

1. Oneness of Allah’s Being

Allah is ‘One’ in His Being. This means:

- When we say Allah is ‘one’, it means that Allah is unique and indivisible.

- Allah is infinite and eternal. He cannot be measured, counted or defined. Allah has no limits because only finite beings have limits. Finite beings have a height, length and depth; and they have a weight, shape and size. But Allah is infinite; He is not limited by either time or space.

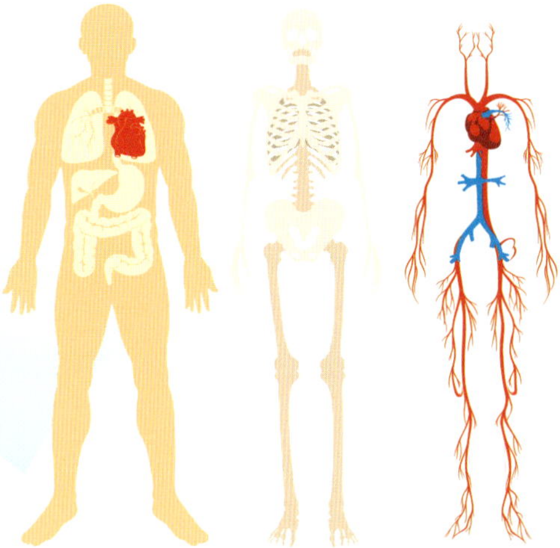

Allah is 'One' - He is not made up of parts or substances. All finite beings and objects are made up of parts and substances: the earth is made up of mountains, seas and land; human beings are made up of muscle, bones and organs; and every natural element is made up of atoms.

Allah is the '**Necessary Being**' (Wajib al-Wujud). A necessary being does not owe its existence to anyone or anything. Everything other than Allah is not necessary; they depend on Allah for their existence.

Allah is unique and incomparable. He does not have a partner or an equal; nor does He have an opposite or a parallel. Allah does not share His divinity and lordship with anyone, because no one is worthy of being worshipped besides Him. This belief is known as **Monotheism** (the belief in the One God).

- Allah does not have a father or mother; and He does not have a wife, son or daughter.

Believing in all of this is tawhid. To believe the opposite of this is shirk, because shirk is the opposite of tawhid. All the following beliefs are shirk:

- To believe someone or something is a partner with Allah. This is known as **Polytheism** (the belief that there is more than one god).
- To believe someone or something is worthy of worship besides Allah. This is known as **Idolatry** (the worship of idols).
- To believe that Allah has a wife, son or daughter.
- To believe Allah has a physical body, such as a three-dimensional shape, or looks like a human being.

2. Oneness of Allah's Attributes

Allah is 'One' in His attributes. This means there is nothing or no one like Him, and nothing is equal to Him. Allah is completely unlike anything in creation and He is greater than anything that we can think of or imagine.

We must know the following:

- Allah is absolute and independent, whereas everything other than Allah is dependent on Him only. To believe this is tawhid; to believe the opposite of this is shirk.

- Allah's attributes are not like human attributes even if they are called by the same names. They are similar in the wording only, and not the meaning. Believing them to mean the same thing would be shirk. For example:

  - Allah is living, and humans are living, but Allah does not need anything, whereas humans need food, water and air to live.

- Allah sees and hears and so do humans, but Allah's sight and hearing has no limitations, but human sight and hearing do have limits.
- Allah has knowledge and humans have knowledge, but Allah's knowledge does not change or increase over time, but human knowledge does change and increase.
- Allah's speech is not like human speech. Humans need sounds, words and language to speak, but Allah's speech is not like this. Only Allah knows the reality of His speech.

All of Allah's attributes are described as having no beginning and no end, unlike the creation, self-sufficient and one. To affirm these for Allah's attributes is tawhid, but to deny anyone of them is shirk.

Believing in these differences between Allah's attributes and human attributes is tawhid and removing them is shirk.

3. Oneness of Allah's Actions

Allah is 'One' in His actions. This means Allah alone is the creator. Nobody else creates anything, not even their own actions. Allah has allowed human beings to make choices, but they cannot bring their choices into action on their own. They need Allah to create their actions for them. This is because everything is done according to Allah's will and power, and only what Allah wants takes place. No one can stop Allah's decision or overrule His judgement.

We must keep the following points in mind:

- Everything takes place only by the will and power of Allah. No one can do anything unless they are given permission by Allah to make it happen. For example, the Prophets perform miracles by Allah's permission and leave. Allah permits them to perform the miracles.

- Everything is absolutely dependant on Him. Nothing has an effect (a result) by its own power. It is Allah Who creates the outcome.

- Every moment of our lives is being created and recreated by Allah. Allah's act of creation never stops and is continuing every moment.

Summary

We must keep in mind that tawhid and shirk are **complete opposites**. When we affirm tawhid, it means that we have rejected shirk. A person cannot be a believer in tawhid and shirk at the same time, just like it cannot be day and night at the same.

Both tawhid and shirk are **systems of belief** and they are not actions that can be practised. Every Muslim in the past and in the present believes in the Oneness of Allah (tawhid). They believe that Allah is one and unique in His being, attributes and actions. They also reject any equality or partnership with Allah in any of these. To call any Muslim a **mushrik** (someone who does shirk) is a major sin in Islam.

Lesson 6

Sirah: The Conquest of Makkah

The Treaty of Hudaybiyah came as a shock to the Muslims. They could not understand why the Prophet ﷺ would agree to this one-sided treaty, which was good for the Quraysh but not for the Muslims. However, they were loyal to the Prophet ﷺ and they learnt to move on from what looked like a bad situation for them.

Allah revealed to the Prophet ﷺ in the Qur'an that this trip to Hudaybiyah was a 'Clear Victory' for the Muslims. It was not long after the Muslims reached Madinah that they started to realise that there were good consequences for the Muslims through this unfair treaty.

Allah Helps the Muslim Prisoners

After arriving in Madinah, the Prophet's Companion Abu Basir escaped from his imprisoners in Makkah and he begged the Prophet ﷺ for protection in

Madinah. Abu Basir was among the Muslims who were imprisoned in Makkah. The Prophet ﷺ told him about the treaty and that he did not want to break its conditions. So, he commanded Abu Basir to return to Makkah with his guards and he told him to remain patient because Allah would find a way out for him. In this way, the Prophet ﷺ followed the Treaty of Hudaybiyah and did not go against its conditions.

When Abu Basir reached a place called Dhu al-Hulayfah, which was a few miles south of Madinah, he thought of a plan to get away from the enemy guards. He asked one of them to show him his sword. The guard agreed, and Abu Basir took the sword and killed the guard and went straight back to the Prophet ﷺ.

Abu Basir said, "O Messenger of Allah, you have kept your promise by handing me over to them." The Prophet ﷺ was surprised by what Abu Basir had done, but he still could not stay in Madinah. So the Prophet ﷺ told the other guard to take Abu Basir back to Makkah, but he was too scared and said that he did not want to.

Because the guard did not want to take him, Abu Basir decided to go and live in a place near the Red Sea. He could not stay in Madinah because of the conditions of the treaty and he did not want to return to his imprisoners in Makkah. So, he lived as a free man without having to follow the Treaty of Hudaybiyah.

The other Muslim prisoners in Makkah heard about what happened with Abu Basir and they wanted to join him. After the treaty, the Quraysh stopped chaining the prisoners in their homes and let them walk around freely in Makkah because they knew that they would be returned to them if they ran away to Madinah. But the Quraysh did not realise that they would run away somewhere else!

Many of the prisoners in Makkah left to join Abu Basir, near the Red Sea. Among them was Abu Jandal, the Companion who had to return to Makkah after the Treaty of Hudaybiyah. These ex-prisoners made a new group of 70 young men who were separate to the city of Madinah, and so they did not have to follow the conditions of the Treaty of Hudaybiyah. They fought against the Quraysh and stopped their trading caravans from reaching Syria. This caused the Quraysh a lot of problems.

The Quraysh got fed up with these young men and they begged the Prophet ﷺ to take them into Madinah. The Prophet ﷺ agreed to this and his prayer for Abu Basir and Abu Jandal was finally answered! Allah had certainly found a way out for them. This was the first victory which Allah promised His Prophet ﷺ after signing the Treaty of Hudaybiyah. Prophet Muhammad ﷺ kept his promise and he did not let the Muslims break their agreement, even if the agreement was with his enemies.

The Arabs are Open to the Message of Islam

As the months went by, the Muslims began to see the good results that the treaty had on their mission to spread Islam. The conditions of the treaty stated that there would be no fighting between the Muslims and the idol worshippers of Makkah. During this time of peace, the Prophet ﷺ sent teachers to all parts of Arabia to invite them to Islam. The Muslims found that the Arabs were open to their message and that they listened to what they had to say. They saw the positive influence of peace because now the Arabs were willing to give Islam a chance. In this short time, many people entered Islam and became Muslims. In fact, more people entered Islam during this short time than in the years before.

The great leader of the Quraysh `Amr bin al-`As and its great commander Khalid bin Walid also became Muslims during this time. This was great news and a big help to the Muslims, because they were important people in Makkah and had a high position among the Quraysh. After the Prophet ﷺ passed away, these two leaders helped Islam greatly; they spread the message of Islam to other parts of the world outside of Arabia. `Amr bin al-`As later became the governor of Egypt and Khalid bin Walid became the most famous Muslim army general.

The Prophet ﷺ also invited the different kings and rulers outside of Arabia to Islam, to show that Islam is for all people, regardless of their race, colour or ethnicity. He sent letters to the Negus (Najashi) of Ethiopia, Heraclius the Caesar of Byzantium, Muqawqis the ruler of Egypt, Chosroes the king of Persia and Harith Gassani, the governor of Syria. He invited all of them to Islam and to accept him as Allah's Final Prophet and Messenger.

The increased conversion to Islam during this period was again another victory that Allah had promised the Prophet ﷺ after the signing of the Treaty of Hudaybiyah.

The Enemy to the North

Thanks to the Treaty of Hudaybiyah, Prophet Muhammad ﷺ did not have to protect Madinah from the Quraysh. He could now concentrate his efforts in defending Madinah against the other enemies.

In the first month of the 7th year after Hijrah, the Prophet ﷺ told the Companions to prepare for an expedition (war). He did not tell his Companions where they were going because it was a secret. When the Muslims started marching, they were pleasantly surprised that they were going to the fortresses of Khaybar.

Khaybar was a place where many of the Jewish tribes now lived. It was in Khaybar that the Banu Nadir tribe had gathered together after they had been thrown out from Madinah. It was from Khaybar that Huyayy bin Akhtab and the other leaders of the Banu Nadir tribe had travelled to Makkah to encourage the Quraysh to attack Madinah in the Battle of Khandaq. These Jewish tribes were a danger to the Muslims.

This is why the Prophet ﷺ wanted to stop them so that they could not harm the Muslims again.

When the Muslims reached Khaybar, they surrounded its fortresses. One by one they kept on conquering the fortresses, and within several weeks they had managed to conquer all of them except one. The Prophet ﷺ said, "Tomorrow, I will give this flag to a man who is loved by Allah and His Prophet. Allah will give the Muslims victory by this man's hands." Everyone went to sleep that night hoping that they would be given the flag the next day.

In the morning, everyone woke up early excited to know who the person was. The Prophet ﷺ called his cousin and son-in-law, `Ali bin Abi Talib, and gave the flag to him. `Ali led the Muslim army and fought bravely. During the battle a Jewish man hit him hard and `Ali's shield fell to the ground. However, `Ali kept on fighting and led the soldiers against the enemy. When he reached the fort, he took a broken door from the side and used it as a shield. He kept fighting and making his way towards the fort, until Allah gave the Muslims victory through him. Khaybar had now been conquered!

After the battle of Khaybar, the Jewish tribes begged the Prophet ﷺ to let them stay in their fortresses instead of having to leave. The Prophet ﷺ allowed them to live in Khaybar in peace on the condition that they give half of their harvest to the Muslims. They were happy with this condition and it made the Muslims wealthy because they had a supply of harvest coming to Madinah each year. The danger from the Jewish tribes in the north had now been removed. This was another victory, which Allah had promised his Prophet ﷺ after signing the Treaty of Hudaybiyah.

The `Umrah Qada'

Later that year, the Muslims returned to Makkah to perform the `Umrah (Minor Pilgrimage). They stayed in Makkah for three days and they performed the

Tawaf around the Ka`bah. When they went to perform the `Umrah, the Muslims were feeling weak because they had suffered from a fever in Madinah, so the Prophet ﷺ ordered the men to uncover their right shoulders (this is known as **Idtiba`**) and to walk like a wrestler in the first three rounds of the Tawaf (this is known as **Raml**). The reason behind the Idtiba` and the Raml was to show the Quraysh that the Muslims were strong and not weak. Today, we do the Idtiba` and Raml during `Umrah to remember this event.

The people of Makkah were impressed by the Muslims. Seeing them perform the `Umrah left a good impression on the hearts of the Arabs. They soon began to realise that Prophet Muhammad ﷺ came with the true religion and that Islam respected the message of their forefather, Prophet Ibrahim عليه السلام. A new respect was developing in their hearts and they began to come even closer to Islam and many of them became Muslims.

The Clear Victory

After seeing the many victories that the Muslims were enjoying such as the conquest of Khaybar to the increased number of people becoming Muslims, the Quraysh soon realised that they were the real losers from the Treaty of Hudaybiyah. Even though at first it looked like the treaty was good for them, it turned out that the Muslims were the ones that really were helped by it. The Treaty of Hudaybiyah was a great success for the Muslims, but the greatest victory was still yet to come.

More than a year after the Treaty of Hudaybiyah had been signed, in the 8th year after Hijrah, the treaty was broken. Some men from the Banu Bakr (the tribe that joined the Quraysh) attacked and killed some people from the Banu Khaza`ah (the tribe that joined the Muslims) in the middle of the night. The Quraysh supported the Banu Bakr in this attack, and therefore they broke the conditions of the treaty by going against their agreement with the Muslims.

By doing this, the Quraysh had ended the Treaty of Hudaybiyah, and this meant that there was no longer peace between them and the Muslims.

When the news of this killing reached the Prophet ﷺ, he was distressed by it. So, he ordered the Muslims to march towards Makkah. The Muslim army had 10,000 soldiers; this was the largest army that the Muslims had ever had. The Quraysh knew that they could not fight back because they had never beaten an army so large. The Quraysh simply watched and worried that their time had come. They knew that they were guilty because they had harmed the Muslims in Makkah and sent armies to attack them in Madinah. What would happen to them now? Would they be punished for their crimes? The day for justice had finally arrived.

The Kind and Merciful Prophet ﷺ

When the Muslims entered Makkah, the Quraysh could not stop them. The Muslim army marched right into Makkah and made its way straight to the Ka`bah. As they were marching, one Companion raised his voice and said, "Today is the day of revenge!" The Prophet ﷺ stopped the Companion, and said, "No, today is the day of mercy!" The Muslim army did not harm any person or attack any home because they were given strict orders not to fight unless they had to in self-defence. This was not a day of war. This was a day of peace.

When the Prophet ﷺ reached the Ka`bah, he performed the Tawaf and he asked for the keys to the Ka`bah to be given to him. When he opened the Ka`bah, he broke all the idols that were inside and commanded that they all be removed. He then stood at the door of the Ka`bah, praised Allah and said, "O Quraysh! Allah has removed ignorance from you and arrogance. All human beings are the children of Prophet Adam عليه السلام, and Prophet Adam عليه السلام was made from clay. O Quraysh! What do you think I will do to you?" "We believe you will be good to us, O generous brother, the son of a generous brother," the Quraysh replied. The Prophet ﷺ showing how kind and merciful he was said, “Go, because you all are free.”

In this single moment, the Prophet ﷺ forgave the Quraysh, who were his enemies for the past 20 years. He did not be arrogant to any of them. He showed them kindness and forgiveness. He remained a humble servant of Allah thanking Him for this great victory.

On this day, Allah fulfilled His promise to His Beloved Prophet ﷺ that was made after signing the Treaty of Hudaybiyah. He had granted him a ‘Clear Victory’ by giving him the conquest of Makkah. Even with all their insults and abuse, the Prophet ﷺ forgave his enemies without holding any bad feelings against them. On this day, the Prophet ﷺ not only conquered Makkah, he also conquered his enemies’ hearts.

Lesson 7

Two Important Types of Sajdah

There are **two** important types of prostration (Sajdah) that we need to know about and they are: the Prostration of Recitation (Sajdat at-Tilawah) and the Prostration of Forgetfulness (Sajdat as-Sahw).

We will discuss both types of Sajdah in the rest of this chapter.

1. The Prostration of Recitation (Sajdat at-Tilawah)

There are **fourteen** verses in the Qur'an where it is necessary (Wajib) on both the reciter and the listener to perform a prostration to Allah. This prostration is known as the 'Prostration of Recitation' (Sajdat at-Tilawah).

How is it Performed?

To perform this prostration, you need to make sure that you are in a state of ritual purity (Taharah) first and that you have not broken your Wudu'. You also must be covered properly.

Once you are ready, stand in the direction of the Qiblah, and go straight down to the prostration position (Sajdah) while saying the takbir (Allahu Akbar). Once you have held your position and have performed the prostration properly, you raise your head from the prostration while saying the takbir (Allahu Akbar), and this completes the prostration.

The Prostration of Recitation (Sajdat at-Tilawah) can also be performed from the sitting position. You do not have to stand up to perform it.

When is it Performed?

The Prostration of Recitation (Sajdat at-Tilawah) can be performed either during the Prayer (Salah), by yourself or behind the Imam, or outside of the prayer.

If a person recites one of the fourteen verses **during the Prayer (Salah)**, he or she must do the prostration straightaway. After performing the prostration, the person will return to the standing position (Qiyam) to continue with their recitation. If the Imam recites the verse, then the Imam will perform the prostration, and everyone behind him will follow him into it.

When not offering the prayer, while sitting down and reciting the Qur'an, the prostration can be performed straight away or at the end of one's recitation. It can also be performed afterwards, but it must not be delayed for too long. Delaying the prostration for no reason is disliked (Makruh).

The Prostration of Recitation (Sajdat at-Tilawah) must be performed after reciting any of the following fourteen verses:

1. Al-A`raf 7:206	2. Al-Ra`d 13:15	3. Al-Nahl 16:50
4. Al-Isra' 17:107	5. Maryam 19:58	6. Al-Hajj 22:18
7. Al-Furqan 25:60	8. Al-Naml 27:25	9. Al-Sajdah 32:15
10. Sad 38:24	11. Fussilat 41:37	12. Al-Najm 53:61
13. Al-Inshiqaq 84:21	14. Al-`Alaq 96:19	

2. The Prostration of Forgetfulness (Sajdat as-Sahw)

During the prayer, sometimes we forget to do something. In these situations, we must make up for that mistake by performing two extra prostrations at the end of the prayer. Performing these two prostrations is called the 'Prostration of Forgetfulness' (Sajdat as-Sawh).

The 'Prostration of Forgetfulness' (Sajdat as-Sawh)

is performed at the end of the prayer when sitting down in the final sitting position (Qa`dah). It is performed in the following way:

1. Recite the Tashahhud (Bearing Witness).
2. Perform the Salam, turning the head to the right side only.
3. Perform two prostrations.
4. Return to the Sitting Position (Qa`dah) and complete the prayer as normal starting from the Tashahhud (Bearing Witness).

When Does the Prostration of Forgetfulness Become Necessary?

To know when it is necessary (Wajib) to perform the 'Prostration of Forgetfulness' (Sajdat as-Sawh), we must first learn about the different grades in the acts of worship. Like the grades of Halal (lawful) and Haram (unlawful), the acts of worship, such as the

Prayer (Salah), Fasting (Sawm) and Pilgrimage (Hajj), also have actions that are graded differently.

In the Prayer (Salah), there are actions that are obligatory (Fard), necessary (Wajib) and recommended (Sunnah). Examples of some of these are given below.

Some of the **obligatory (Fard)** actions of the Salah, of which some are 'conditions' of the prayer (shurut) and others are its 'pillars' (arkan), are the following:

1. Having purification (Taharah) of the body, clothes and place
2. Facing the Qiblah
3. Covering the nakedness (`awrah)
4. Intention (Niyyah)
5. Tahrimah
6. Standing Position (Qiyam)
7. Reciting the Qur'an (even one verse)

8. Bowing Position (Ruku`)

9. Prostration Position (Sajdah)

10. The final Sitting Position (Qa`dah al-Akhirah)

Some of the **necessary (Wajib)** actions of the Salah are the following:

1. Reciting Surat al-Fatihah

2. Reciting a short Surah or three verses

3. Performing the second prostration (Sajdah) before starting the next unit

4. Standing after Ruku' (i.e. the Qawmah)

5. Sitting in between the two prostrations (i.e., the Jalsah)

6. The first Sitting Position (Qa`dah)

7. Keeping the right order between the actions

8. Reciting Tashahhud in the first and last sitting position

9. Saying the word ‘Salam’ to complete the prayer
10. Reciting the Qunut Supplication in the Witr prayer

Some of the **recommended (Sunnah)** actions of the Salah are the following:

1. Thana’
2. Ta`awwudh
3. Tasmiyah
4. Saying ‘Amin’
5. Takbir of Ruku’
6. Tasbih of Ruku` (three times)
7. Takbir of Sajdah
8. Tasbih of Sajdah (three times)
9. Pointing the finger during the Tashahhud
10. The Salat al-Ibrahimiyyah

11. The Du`a

If you miss any of the **obligatory (Fard)** actions of the prayer, the prayer (Salah) is **invalid**, and it will have to be performed again. For example, if you broke your Wudu' during the prayer, turned away from the Qibla or forgot to do a Ruku` or Sujud, then the prayer is invalid, and it will have to be repeated.

If you miss any of the **recommended (Sunnah)** actions of the prayer, the prayer (Salah) will be **imperfect**, however it will still be valid. For example, forgetting to raise the finger during the Tashahhud or forgetting to say the takbir (Allahu Akbar) when going into the Ruku` or Sajdah does not make the prayer invalid. The prayer is imperfect, but it is still valid. It does NOT need to be repeated.

The **necessary (Wajib)** actions, however, are in between the obligatory (Fard) and the recommended (Sunnah) actions. If it is missed **on purpose**, the prayer is **incomplete**, and it must be performed again. But if it is missed **forgetfully**, then the person can perform the 'Prostration of Forgetfulness' (Sajdat as-Sahw) to make up for the incomplete part of the prayer.

If several Wajib actions were missed, **one** Sajdat as-Sahw would suffice for all of them (i.e. a seperate Sajdat as-Sahw does not need to be done for each of them).

In conclusion, the 'Prostration of Forgetfulness' (Sajdat as-Sahw) is performed when missing a **necessary (Wajib)** action of the prayer **forgetfully**. There is no such prostration for missing the obligatory (Fard) or recommended (Sunnah) actions of the prayer.

Lesson 8

Prophets Represent Human Perfection

Flint, coal, basalt, limestone, diamond, emerald and ruby are all stones, but they are NOT all equal. The last three are not just stones, but they are '**precious stones**', known as gems and jewels. Similarly, the Prophets are human beings, but they are special human beings. They have been chosen by Allah to be His representatives and ambassadors on earth.

Basalt

Limestone

Ruby

Diamond

The Prophets are not supernatural beings, such as the angels, but they are the most perfect human beings. They are the best among humanity who have the most excellent examples of human behaviour. In the Qur'an, Allah commands us that if we want to be close to Him, then we must walk in the footsteps of Prophet Muhammad ﷺ (al-Ahzab 33:21). This is because the Prophet ﷺ is not an ordinary human being like us, but he is the most perfect human being who has the best example and most beautiful character.

The Superiority of the Prophets

Allah made the Prophets superior over all people. They are the best of humanity. Ibn `Abbas reports that some of the Companions were sitting and waiting for the Prophet ﷺ. When the Prophet ﷺ came towards them, he heard them having a conversation. One of them said, "How amazing it is that Allah chose a dear friend from among His creation! He chose Ibrahim عليه السلام as a dear friend." Another said, "What is more amazing than the speaking of Musa عليه السلام? Allah spoke to him directly." Another said, "`Isa عليه السلام is the Word of Allah and His Spirit." Another said, "Adam عليه السلام was chosen by Allah."

The Prophet ﷺ approached them, greeted them and said, "I heard your discussion and your amazement that Ibrahim عليه السلام is **Allah's Dear Friend (Khalil Allah)** for that is how he is, and that Musa عليه السلام is **Allah's Confidant (Najiyy Allah)** for that is how he is, and that `Isa عليه السلام is **Allah's Spirit and His Word (Ruh Allah wa Kalimatuhu)** for that is how he is, and that Adam عليه السلام was **Chosen by Allah (Safiyy Allah)**, for that is how he is. Listen! I am indeed **the Beloved**

of Allah (Habib Allah) and that is no boast." (at-Tirmidhi)

The Prophets are the Most Honourable

The Prophets were the most respected and honourable people within their communities. However, when they brought Allah's message, their people rejected them only because they did not want to follow their teachings. For example, Allah mentions the reaction of Prophet Salih's people: *"They said: 'O Salih, you have been the centre of hope amongst our people before this.'"* (Hud 11:62) Prophet Salih's people recognised his superiority, but they turned away from him only because they were not ready to accept his message.

The Prophets were born into honourable families with the best family line. Abu Hurayra reports that the Prophet ﷺ said, "I was raised from the best of each generation of the children of Adam." (al-Bukhari).

Wathila bin al-Asqa` also reports that the Prophet ﷺ said, "Allah chose **Kinana** from the children of

Isma'il, and He chose the **Quraysh** from among the Kinana, and He chose **Banu Hashim** amongst the Quraysh, and He chose **me** from the Banu Hashim." (Muslim)

The Incomparability of the Prophets

The Prophets have no equal among humankind. They are the best human beings who cannot be compared to. They have the finest inner and outer qualities.

Regarding Prophet Muhammad's **inner qualities**, Anas said, "The Prophet ﷺ was the best of all the people in conduct and behaviour." (al-Bukhari and Muslim)

When someone asked the Mother of the Believers `A'isha about the Prophet's character, she asked, "Have you not read the Qur'an?" "Yes," replied the person. "For verily, the Prophet's character was the Qur'an." (Ahmad)

The Prophet ﷺ also had the best **outward**

qualities. Al-Bara' said, "The Prophet ﷺ was the most handsome of all the people and had the best appearance. He was neither very tall nor short." (al-Bukhari and Muslim)

`Ali said, "I have never seen the likes of him before or after. May my mother and father be sacrificed for him." (Ahmad and at-Tirmidhi)

Describing the special features of the Prophet ﷺ, Ibn `Abbas said, "When the Prophet ﷺ spoke, a light came from between his teeth." (ad-Darimi)

Hind bin Abi Hala said, "The Prophet ﷺ was majestic and he was held in great esteem. His blessed face shone like the full moon." (at-Tabarani)

In one narration, Anas said, "I have not touched silk or a silk garment softer than the palm of the Prophet ﷺ, nor have I smelt a perfume nicer than the sweat of the Prophet ﷺ." (al-Bukhari and Muslim)

And in another narration, he reports: "The Prophet ﷺ had a very fair skin tone and the drops of his sweat shone like pearls." (Muslim)

The Prophets are Law-Givers

The Prophets are Allah's **representatives** and **ambassadors** to humanity. They speak on Allah's authority and by His permission. They have the duty of explaining Allah's laws to their people and showing them how to practice them. No other human being has this power, as every human being is commanded by Allah to follow the Prophets. No one is allowed to reject or change the laws given by the Prophets.

The Prophets do not just explain Allah's laws; they also have the power to give new laws from themselves. For example, Prophet Muhammad ﷺ made Madinah a holy city (Haram) like the way Makkah was made a holy city (Haram) by Prophet Ibrahim عليه السلام (al-Bukhari and Muslim). The Prophet ﷺ also made fish lawful (halal) for his Ummah even though it is not sacrificed, and it dies when it is taken out of the water (Ibn Majah).

The words and actions of Prophet Muhammad ﷺ are known as his '**Sunnah**'. Many of the Islamic laws are based on the Sunnah of the Prophet ﷺ. The Qur'an did not explain everything in detail, as it left many things for the Prophet ﷺ to explain through his Sunnah. For example, Allah commanded us to pray in the Qur'an, but He did not explain how. The Prophet ﷺ showed his Ummah how to pray, and they learnt to pray by watching him.

In this way, the Prophet's Sunnah is the **practical demonstration** of the Qur'an. Just as it is obligatory to follow the Qur'an, it is also obligatory to follow the Sunnah of Prophet Muhammad ﷺ.

Summary

The Prophets are special servants of Allah and the most perfect human beings. They are unlike other humans in their inward and outward reality. They have been given superiority by Allah over all of humanity. They are the most honourable and respected among their people and they come from the best families. They also have a special status as law-givers because they can give laws and explain them by the authority of Allah.

Lesson 9

Other Types of Salah (Part 1)

There are other types of Prayer (Salah) that are important for us to know about. We will go through some of them below.

1. The Qada' Prayer

Performing the prayer on time is known as **`Ada**. There are times when you might miss the prayer unintentionally, such as forgetting or falling asleep. Making up a missed prayer is known as **Qada'**. The prayers that have been missed are like a debt that needs to be repaid. By performing the Qada' prayer, you are making up for the missed prayer and fulfilling your duty to Allah.

The Qada' prayer is performed like the normal prayer except that it is performed after the prayer time has ended. Only the missed **Fard** and **Witr (Wajib)** prayers are performed in the Qada' prayer. **Sunnah** and **Nafl** prayers are not made up as Qada'.

When performing the Qada' prayer, you must specify in the intention the missed prayer that you are making up for. So, if you missed the Fajr prayer, then in the Qada' prayer, you need to specify in the intention that you are making up the missed Fajr prayer.

If you miss a prayer, you should make up for it straightaway as soon as you remember. You should perform it as Qada' before starting the next Fard prayer, as long as there is enough time to do so. However, missing the prayer is a major sin. The Qada' only makes up for the obligation; it does not remove the sin of missing the prayer on purpose.

If you have missed less than **six** prayers, you should keep the order of the prayers when you perform them as Qada'. For example, if you missed the Fajr, Zuhr and `Asr prayers then when you make up for them they should be performed in the same order, i.e. Fajr first, then Zuhr and then `Asr.

2. The Sick Person's Prayer

When a person is sick or ill, they are not excused from praying; they still need to pray to the best of their ability.

If a person cannot stand up due to weakness or finds it painful to do so, then they should sit down on the floor and pray whilst sitting down.

They should sit on the floor in the Qa`dah (Sitting Position) as they do in the prayer normally, but if this is too difficult, then they can sit in any position that they find comfortable. The Ruku' (Bowing Position) and the Sajdah (Prostration) can be performed from the sitting position. If a person can stand but cannot perform the Ruku' (Bowing Position) and the Sajdah (Prostration) properly, then he or she can pray sitting down as well.

If someone cannot perform the Ruku' (Bowing Position) and the Sajdah (Prostration) due to weakness or pain, they can perform it by performing head movements. In this case the Ruku' (Bowing

Position) can be performed by lowering the head a little bit and the Sajdah (Prostration) can be performed by lowering the head a little further down.

If someone cannot sit up due to weakness, they can pray whilst lying down on their back. The legs should face the Qiblah, but the knees should be raised so that the feet do not face the Qiblah.

If it is difficult to raise the knees, then it can be performed without raising them. The Ruku' (Bowing Position) and the Sajdah (Prostration) can be performed by making small movements with the head. In this case the Ruku' (Bowing Position) can be performed by lowering the head a little and the Sajdah (Prostration) can be performed by lowering the head a little lower.

If a person cannot lie on their back, then they can lie on their side and pray in this position with the head movements. It is better to lie down on the right side than the left, but if it is difficult, either side is acceptable.

3. The Traveller's Prayer

There is a different ruling for the prayer when we are travelling and away from home. We shorten the four units of the Fard prayers and perform them as two units. This prayer, which is performed by the traveller, is called '**Qasr**'.

The traveller will perform the following **Fard** prayers while he or she is away from home:

Prayer	Fajr	Zuhr	`Asr	Maghrib	`Isha'
Resident's Prayer	2 Fard	4 Fard	4 Fard	3 Fard	4 Fard
Traveller's Prayer	2 Fard	2 Fard	2 Fard	3 Fard	2 Fard

NOTE: The traveller has a choice to perform the **Sunnah** and **Nafl** prayers, but the **Witr (Wajib)** prayer must be performed as normal.

A person becomes a traveller, if he or she intends to travel for **48 miles** or more plans to stay at the destination for **less than 15 days**. During these days, he or she will shorten the four units of the Fard prayers and offer them as Qasr.

The Qasr prayer can be performed as soon as a person leaves their town or city, while they are travelling.

During this time, if a person offers the prayer behind an Imam who is not a traveller, then the traveller must offer the prayer in full and not as Qasr. However, if the prayer is missed, then it must be made up as Qasr, even if the traveller has returned home and is no longer a traveller.

If a person plans to stay at their destination for **15 days or more**, they are not considered to be a traveller and they must perform the prayers in full. They can perform the Qasr prayer while travelling before reaching the destination.

Praying While Travelling

When we are travelling on the motorway, we must stop the car in a safe place such as a service station and pray outside of the car by facing the Qiblah.

We are not allowed to perform the **Fard** or **Witr (Wajib)** prayer in the car seat, because the Qiyam (the Standing Position) needs to be performed and this can only be done while being outside of the car. In some service stations, facilities have been provided for the prayer such as prayer rooms.

The prayer can be performed on a plane. When we pray on a plane, we must follow the timings of the country that we are flying over and not the timings of our home country or the country we are travelling to. You can find out the prayer time by looking at the position of the sun in the sky or you can ask the aircrew for the timing of the prayer.

We must perform the prayer as normal, but if someone has an excuse, such as feeling dizzy or lack of space, then the prayer can be performed in the sitting position (on the floor of the plane).

If it is not possible to perform the prayer either standing or sitting while facing the Qiblah, then it can be performed whilst sitting down in the seat facing any direction. In this case you can make head movements for the Ruku` (Bowing Position) and Sajdah (Prostration). But this prayer will have to be repeated when getting off the plane, because it was not performed properly.

Lesson 10

Sirah: The Farewell Pilgrimage

It was the 20th of Ramadan 8 AH (After Hijrah) when the Muslims conquered Makkah. This conquest was the 'Clear Victory' that Allah had promised His Prophet ﷺ after signing the Treaty of Hudaybiyah. This treaty initially came as a shock to the Muslims because it was a one-sided treaty and it had favoured the Quraysh.

The Companions initially thought that the treaty was bad for the Muslims. However, they did not know that in less than two years after signing it that they would be marching peacefully into Makkah with an army of 10,000 men. This peaceful conquest showed the world that Prophet Muhammad ﷺ was a great political leader who always chose peace over war.

The Quraysh Accept Islam

After the conquest, the many people of Makkah accepted Islam. Allah revealed a whole chapter in the Qur'an about this: "*When there comes Allah's help and victory, and you see people joining Allah's Din (Religion) in crowds. Then glorify Allah's praise (in gratitude), exalting Him, and beg Him (humbly) for pardon. Surely, He is Ever-Relenting and Oft-Returning (with evermore compassion)."* (an-Nasr 110:1-3)

The Quraysh were the leading tribe in Arabia, and after they accepted Islam, many of the Arab tribes that followed them also entered Islam without a question. The Prophet ﷺ sent teachers to all the new tribes to teach them about Islam. The Banu Hawazin tribe and its allies, however, saw themselves as rivals to the Quraysh. They belonged to the city of Ta'if and its surrounding areas. This tribe did not want to accept Islam, so they gathered a large army and marched towards Makkah.

The Battle of Hunayn

When the Prophet ﷺ found out about the advancing army from Ta'if, he set out from Makkah with an army of 12,000 men (10,000 from before the conquest of Makkah and another 2000 from the Quraysh). The

Muslims were proud of their strength and believed that they could not be defeated on this day, because they had such a large army. When the Muslims arrived at a place called Hunayn, 4000 men from the Banu Hawazin were hiding and waiting to surprise the Muslim army with an attack. As the Muslims were passing through a narrow path, the Banu Hawazin attacked the Muslims with stones and arrows which left the Muslim army confused.

Many soldiers ran away from the battle because they were afraid that they would be killed. But the Prophet ﷺ was not afraid. He called his closest Companions to gather around him and to face the enemy. With great courage and bravery, the Prophet ﷺ went straight towards the enemy followed by the Companions around him. He recited the following words to show his enemies that he was not afraid:

أَنَا النَّبِيُّ لَا كَذِبْ
أَنَا ابْنُ عَبْدِ الْمُطَّلِبْ

I am truly the Prophet
I am the son of `Abd al-Muttalib

The Prophet ﷺ prayed to Allah to send down His help. The Muslims fought with complete determination and it was not long before they defeated the Banu Hawazin. The Battle of Hunayn came to an end! Many of the enemy soldiers tried to escape but they were followed until they were caught.

After the battle of Hunayn, many of the people from the Banu Hawazin became Muslims. The people in the areas nearby Ta'if accepted Islam, but the people of Ta'if did not and they blocked the entry into the city. The Muslims surrounded Ta'if but they were unable to conquer it. So, the Prophet ﷺ commanded the Muslims to return home.

The Expedition to Tabuk

A few months later, news reached the Prophet ﷺ that the Byzantines were sending a great army to attack Madinah. The Byzantines were Christians. A year earlier before the conquest of Makkah, the Byzantine with the Ghassanids (an Arab Christian empire that was in the north of Arabia) had sent an army of

10,000 people to fight the Muslims at a place called Mu`tah (in Jordan). The Muslims fought with them for three days but were unable to reach victory. On the third day of the battle, when the fighting got worse and some of the Muslim commanders were killed, the Muslim army planned its way out of the battlefield and returned to Madinah.

Now, a year later in the 9th year after Hijrah, the Byzantines were returning with an even greater army to bring an end to Islam. So, the Prophet ﷺ gathered the Muslims together to march northwards towards Syria. When the Muslim army reached a place called Tabuk (north of Arabia), they waited for the Byzantine army, but they did not appear. The Muslim army went to the borders of Syria and this frightened the Byzantines, and the Byzantines did not come out to fight.

The news that the Byzantine army did not come to fight, sent a strong message to the other Arab tribes in the north. The Byzantines were the superpower in those days and many people now thought that the Muslim army was greater than them and so they turned their backs on the Byzantines and accepted to work with the Muslims instead. This helped to connect many of the Christian Arab tribes in the north of Arabia to Madinah, and it brought the border of the Muslim lands up to Syria which was right next to the Byzantine Empire.

The bravery of the Muslims to stand up to the superpower of the day increased the good position of the Muslims in Arabia. One by one representatives were sent to Madinah from different tribes all over Arabia to accept Islam and to declare that all the members of their tribes had become Muslims. The Arabs believed that if Prophet Muhammad ﷺ was speaking the truth, Allah would give him victory over his enemies and make Islam the main religion. So after seeing all the great victories by the Muslims, the Arabs accepted Islam as their religion. They finally came to recognise that Prophet Muhammad ﷺ was truly Allah's Prophet.

For the first time in history, Arabia was united under a single leader. The people of Ta'if also came to accept Islam. They were no longer able to keep the

Muslims away, because all the lands surrounding them had converted to Islam. They felt that they had to give themselves up to the Muslims. The Prophet ﷺ accepted their embracing Islam and commanded them to destroy the statue of the false goddess al-Lat, to which they unwillingly agreed. One by the one the places of idol worship were being destroyed, and the true worship of the One God was spreading throughout Arabia.

The Farewell Sermon

As the months passed by, the Muslims continued to get stronger and grow even larger in numbers. When the Prophet ﷺ announced that he would perform the Hajj (Major Pilgrimage), 124,000 people were ready to join him. The Prophet's Hajj, which took place at the end of the 10th year after Hijrah, is known as the Farewell Pilgrimage (Hajjat al-Wada`) because it was the last and only Pilgrimage performed by the Prophet ﷺ.

During the Hajj, the Prophet ﷺ delivered a special message at `Arafat. This special message is known as the **'Farewell Sermon' (Khutbat al-Wada`)**. The Farewell Sermon is a very important speech because in it the Prophet ﷺ talks about human respect and equality. The Prophet ﷺ explained what the rights of people are, and how Islam can create peace and justice on the earth.

In this sermon, the Prophet ﷺ first spoke about every person's **right to life** and to their belongings. He said, "O people, listen to my words for I do not know whether I shall ever meet you again in this place after this year. Just as you see this day, this month and this city as being holy, also see your blood and wealth as a holy trust until you meet your Lord. Surely, you will meet your Lord and He will ask you about your deeds. I have already told you about this."

The Prophet ﷺ then stopped all **unfair practices** to do with money, belongings and business, telling everyone to be fair in everything that they do. He said, "Whoever is looking after something for someone else, let him return it to the one who trusted him with it. You can take back the money you borrowed to others, but you cannot charge them for it. Do not mistreat others and you shall not be mistreated."

In this sermon, the Prophet ﷺ talked about **women's rights**. He said, "O people, it is true that you have a right over your wives, but they also have a right over you. Fear Allah and treat women well, for they are your partners and committed helpers, and they do not have anything for themselves. You have taken them only as a trust from Allah, and you have made the enjoyment of their persons lawful by the word of Allah, so understand and listen to my words."

The Prophet ﷺ also spoke about **the equality of all human beings**. He said, "All human beings are the children of Adam and Hawwa'. No Arab is better than a non-Arab and no non-Arab is better than an Arab. No white person is better than a black person and no black person is better than a white person. A person is only better than another person in piety and good conduct."

The Prophet ﷺ then gave some **final words of guidance** saying, "O people, there will be NO prophet after me and no nation will come after you. So, worship your Lord, pray your five daily prayers, fast in the month of Ramadan, give your Zakah freely, perform the Hajj to the Holy House of your Lord and obey those who are in charge of you, so that you may enter Your Lord's Paradise (Jannah)."

Then the Prophet ﷺ said, "O people, I have given the Message, and have left you with something which, if you hold on to it, you will never be misguided or go astray: The **Book of Allah** and the **Sunnah of His Prophet**. Listen to my words, O people, for I have passed on the message so understand it. You should know that every Muslim is a brother of another Muslim, and that all Muslims are brothers. It is not allowed for a person to take from his brother except that which he has given him freely, so do not wrong yourselves."

Then the Prophet ﷺ looked up to the heavens and prayed, "O Allah, have I not carried the message?" And the people said, "O Allah, yes," and the Prophet ﷺ said, "O Allah, bear witness."

The Prophet ﷺ then commanded those Muslims who were there to tell those who were not there about the farewell sermon. As soon as the Prophet ﷺ had completed his Farewell Sermon Allah revealed the Quranic verse of the '**Completion of the Religion**': *"Today I have perfected your Din (Religion) for you, and have completed My Blessing upon you, and have chosen for you Islam (as a) Din (a complete code of life)."* (al-Ma'idah 5:3)

This verse of the Qur'an showed that the Prophet's mission was complete. He had achieved the goal that was set out for him by Allah. Islam was chosen as the FINAL religion for humankind and NO prophet would be born after Prophet Muhammad ﷺ and NO holy book would be revealed after the Qur'an.

Islam was now complete, and it was the final and perfect source of guidance for all of humankind till the Day of Judgement. Anyone who claims to be a prophet after this day is a liar.

The Prophet ﷺ Returns to His Lord

In the 11th year after Hijrah, three months after the Farewell Pilgrimage, the Prophet ﷺ fell ill. During his illness, the Prophet ﷺ stayed in the house of his beloved wife `A'isha. The Prophet ﷺ ordered his best friend and closest Companion Abu Bakr to lead the prayers in his mosque. Days passed by and the Prophet ﷺ did not come out of the house. He was still suffering from the illness and remained at home.

On one of the days, the Prophet ﷺ felt a little better. He got up from his bed and lifted the curtain that separated his house from the mosque. He saw his Companions praying together with Abu Bakr as their leader. Seeing this made the Prophet ﷺ smile. As the Prophet ﷺ was looking at them, the Companions noticed the glowing and illuminating light from the face of the Prophet ﷺ. In excitement they turned their faces to him and were about to break their rows of prayer.

Abu Bakr as-Siddiq moved back to the first row thinking that the Prophet ﷺ would now lead them in prayer, but the Prophet ﷺ signalled to them to continue with their prayer and he did not tell them to repeat it. Then he went behind the curtain again (al-Bukhari). This showed that the Prophet ﷺ was happy with his Companions, and that he was pleased seeing them being led by Abu Bakr as-Siddiq.

This was the last time the Companions saw the Prophet ﷺ. Later that day, on Monday 12th Rabi` al-Awwal 11 AH, the Prophet ﷺ passed away. He died whilst laying in the lap of his beloved wife and the Mother of the Believers `A'isha. The Companions were really saddened by this news and they could not believe it. Anas bin Malik said that when the Prophet ﷺ entered Madinah after his emigration, everything became full of light, but when he passed away everything became darkened (at-Tirmidhi). The Prophet's passing from this world was a great loss for the Companions, and many of them could not smile or be happy again.

Passing on the Light of Islam

The Companions continued with the Prophet's mission to call the whole world to Islam. They continued passing on his message and struggling for the cause of Islam so much that within 30 years, the Islamic borders reached past Arabia. The Muslims conquered Syria and Palestine, and brought the first Qibla of Islam, Masjid al-Aqsa, which is in Palestine, under Islamic rule. They also conquered Egypt, Persia (Iran and Iraq) and North Africa. Allah's promise to Prophet Muhammad ﷺ that Islam will spread to the east and the west was fulfilled within a short time after he passed away.

The light of Islam continued to shine throughout the centuries. Today, there are almost 2 billion Muslims and one in every four people in the world is a Muslim. Islam is on the way to becoming the largest religion! There is not a country on the earth except that the five daily prayers are performed and the Adhan is recited. This is the everlasting impact of the efforts made by Prophet Muhammad ﷺ and his Companions more than 1400 years ago.

Lesson 11

Virtues and Miracles of Prophet Muhammad ﷺ

Prophet Muhammad ﷺ is Allah's beloved and His best creation. Let us learn about his virtues and miracles.

The Virtues of Prophet Muhammad ﷺ

In several narrations, the Prophet ﷺ described his qualities and excellence. Various Companions narrated that the Prophet ﷺ said:

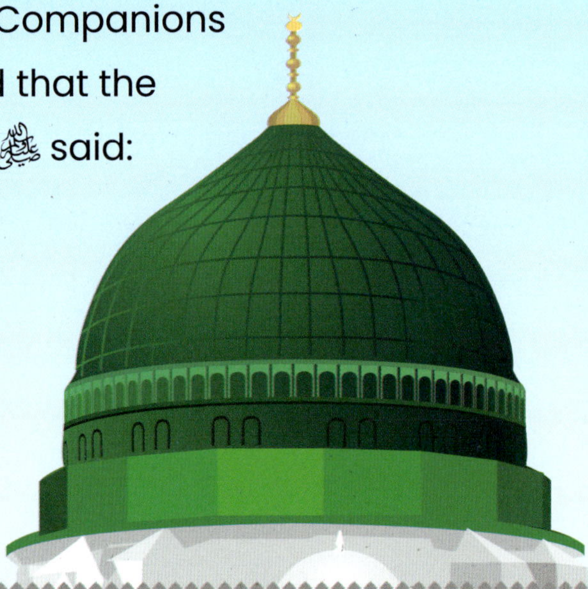

"I have five names: I am **Muhammad** (the praiseworthy) and **Ahmad** (the highly praised or the one who is most praised); I am **al-Mahi** (the eraser) with whom Allah erases unbelief; I am **al-Hashir** (the collector) at whose feet the people will be gathered; and I am **al-`Aqib** (the last in the succession of Prophets)."
(al-Bukhari and Muslim)

"I am the **bearer of the banner of praise** on the Day of Resurrection, and that is no boast. I will be the **first to knock the gate of Paradise**, for Allah will open the gate for me then He will allow me to enter it accompanied by the poor believers, and that is no boast. I am **the noblest of the first and the last** and that is no boast."
(at-Tirmidhi)

"I will be the **first** of them to come forth (from the grave). I will be their **leader** when they will be assembled. I will be their **spokesman** when they will be quiet. I will be their **intercessor** when they will be judged, and I will be **the one who brings them glad tidings** when they are in despair. Nobility and the keys of Paradise will be in my hands on that Day, for I am the noblest of the children of Adam in the sight of my Lord." (at-Tirmidhi)

"When the Day of Judgement comes, I will be the **leader of the Prophets** and the one who addresses them, and the one among them who will agree to intercede, and it is no boast. (at-Tirmidhi and Ibn Majah)"

> I have been given superiority over the other Prophets in **six** respects: (1) I have been given words which are short but complete in meaning; (2) I have been helped by awe (in the hearts of enemies); (3) gains of war have been made lawful to me: (4) the earth has been made clean for me and a place of worship; (5) I have been sent to all mankind and (6) the line of prophets is closed with me. (Muslim)

The Last and Final Prophet

Among the qualities and excellence of Prophet Muhammad ﷺ is that he is the **last and final Prophet of Allah**. There will NOT be another prophet after him. To believe otherwise is to reject this well-established quality of Prophet Muhammad ﷺ, and this amounts to disbelief.

Prophet Muhammad ﷺ is a Prophet for everyone. Allah commanded the Prophet ﷺ to declare: "*Say: 'O humankind! I have (come) to all of you (as) the Messenger of Allah.'*" (al-A`raf 7:158) Explaining this, Jabir bin `Abd Allah narrates that the Prophet ﷺ said, "Every Prophet used to be sent to his nation only, but I have been sent to ALL humankind." (al-Bukhari)

As Prophet Muhammad ﷺ was the last and final Prophet, he was sent for all people and for all ages. His prophethood includes all nations, ethnicities and races, and it is not restricted to one nation or time. Allah has perfected the religion through him and there is no need for any new prophet after him. In the Qur'an, Allah says, "*This day I have perfected your religion for you and completed My favour unto you and have chosen for you Islam as your religion.*" (al-Ma'idah 5:3)

Allah has stated clearly in the Qur'an that Prophet Muhammad ﷺ is His last and final Prophet and

Messenger. He says, "*Muhammad ﷺ is not the father of any of your men, but he is the Messenger of Allah and the Last of the Prophets (ending the chain of the Prophets). And Allah is the Perfect Knower of everything.*" (al-Ahzab 33:40)

Prophet Muhammad ﷺ also made it clear that he is the last Prophet and that there will NOT be any new prophet after him. He said:

1. "My likeness and the likeness of the Prophets before me is the same as the likeness of a man who built a house, then decorated it and beautified it, but left the last brick in a corner, so the people started surrounding the last brick and admiring it, saying, 'Why has this brick not been placed?' He said, 'I am that final piece and I am the **Seal (Finality) of the Prophets (Khatam al-Nabiyyin)**.'" (al-Bukhari and Muslim)

2. "The Children of Isra'il were ruled over by the Prophets. When one Prophet died, another

succeeded him; but after me there is NO prophet but there will be **caliphs**." (al-Bukhari and Muslim)

3. "The Day of Judgement will not be established until there will be **thirty major liars** in my Ummah, each of them claiming to be a prophet. I am the **Seal (Finality) of the Prophets (Khatam an-Nabiyyin)** and there is NO prophet after me." (at-Tirmidhi)

Miracles

The Qur'an is the greatest miracle of Prophet Muhammad ﷺ. Other great miracles were the 'Splitting of the Moon' and the 'Night Journey and the Heavenly Ascension' (al-Isra' wa'l-Mi`raj). However, the Prophet ﷺ had many other miracles as well. Some of these are mentioned below.

1. Commanding the Rains

Anas bin Malik narrates: While the Prophet ﷺ was

delivering a sermon on a Friday, a man stood up and said, "O Allah's Messenger! Pray to Allah to bless us with rain." The Prophet ﷺ raised his hands and no sooner did he do that than the sky became overcast and it started raining so much that people could only just reach their homes. It kept on raining till the next Friday when the same man (or another man) got up and said, "Pray to Allah to withhold the rain from us, for we have been drowned (with heavy rain)." The Prophet ﷺ said, "O Allah! Let it rain around us and not on us." Then the clouds started scattering around Madinah and the rain stopped falling on the people of Madinah. (al-Bukhari)

2. Creating Water

Jabir bin `Abd Allah narrates: The people felt thirsty on the Day of al-Hudaybiyah and there was a small flask of water lying in front of the Prophet ﷺ and he performed the ablution. The people rushed towards him, so he asked, "What is the matter with you?" The

Companions said, "O Messenger of Allah, we have no water with which to perform the ablution, nor any to drink, except what is lying with you." (Upon hearing this,) he put his hand into the flask. Water began to gush out between his fingers like fountains, so we drank till we were full, and we performed ablution as well. Salim bin Abi al-Ja`d asked, "How many were you?" Jabir bin `Abd Allah said, "If we had been a hundred thousand, it would have still been enough, but we were only fifteen hundred." (al-Bukhari)

3. Commanding the Mountains

Anas bin Malik narrates: "The Prophet ﷺ once climbed the mountain of Uhud with Abu Bakr, `Umar and `Uthman. The mountain shook. The Prophet ﷺ said (to the mountain), "Be firm, O Uhud! For on you there are no more than a Prophet, a Siddiq and two martyrs." (al-Bukhari)

4. Seeking Blessings from His Cloak

`Abd Allah, the freed slave of Asma', narrates: I went to Asma' (the sister of `A'isha) and she said: "Here is the cloak of Allah's Messenger ﷺ. This was with `A'isha until she died, and when she died, I got it. The Prophet ﷺ used to wear it, and we soak it in water and give (the water) to the sick. (This is how) we seek cure through it to make them better." (Muslim)

5. Seeking Blessings from His Grave

Abu al-Jawza' Aws bin `Abd Allah narrates: "The people of Madinah were stricken by a severe drought. The people complained to `A'isha. She said, 'Look at the grave of the Prophet ﷺ and make an opening in the roof, so that there is no covering between the grave and the sky. They did this, and it began to rain abundantly until the grass grew and the camels became so fat that it seemed like they would burst. This year was known as the **Year of Abundance**." (ad-Darimi)

Lesson 12

The Divine Decree

We must believe in the **Divine Decree (qadar)**. This means that Allah has perfect knowledge about everything before it is created by Him and He creates that thing in accordance to that knowledge. Thus, good and bad, happiness or sorrow, pleasure or pain, all comes from Allah Almighty.

The Divine Decree (qadar) is Allah's **secret**. No one knows its reality — not even the greatest angels or the mightiest messengers. Anyone who tries to understand it will become confused.

If Allah wills something to happen, it will take place as He commanded, and if He wills for it not to happen, it will not take place, no matter how much a person wants it.

Everyone must submit themselves before Allah and accept the fate with which he or she has been given. We need to take responsibility for our own decisions. Allah says that "*He cannot be questioned for what He does but they will be questioned (for every action that they do).*" (al-Anbiya' 21:23)

Free Will and Human Responsibility

Allah has blessed human beings with **free will**. Free will is the ability to make your choice to do something without being forced to do it. Allah gave human beings free will so that they may be tested in this life to see who the best in character will be (al-Mulk 67:2)

Free will is what gives human beings superiority over the angels. It is certainly a great **responsibility**, because Allah will question us on the choices that we make, and He will judge our actions, giving us either punishment or reward.

Human beings are not forced by Allah to do either good or bad; it is the person's own choosing. We cannot blame Allah for our bad actions, because only we are to blame for the bad consequences of our actions. Allah simply creates our actions according to our choices.

We must never lose sight that this life is only a **test**, because our real life is in the hereafter. This worldly life is only a preparation for the life to come. This is the reason why there are difficulties and suffering in this world, because Allah is testing us to show who is the best in behaviour and conduct.

Allah created this world in such a way that there are times of comfort and times of difficulty. When we are going through hard times, we must not lose faith or hope but we should try to get closer to Allah by being His devoted and sincere servants.

We may not know the reason behind the difficulties and hard times that we face, but we must trust in Allah's plan. No difficulty or hardship happens to us except that there is some good hidden in it.

Whatever we go through in this life, by having true faith in Allah and complete trust in Him, we get a greater benefit either in this life or in the next life.

Everything Good and Bad is from Allah

Allah is the creator of both good and bad. They are both His creations and under His perfect power and control. Nothing is good or bad for Allah, because nothing can benefit Him or bring Him harm. Human beings, on the other hand, want the good because it helps them, and they stay away from the bad because it harms them.

All of Allah's actions are good, because they are expressions of His **mercy** or **justice**. None of Allah's actions are bad, because it is impossible for Allah to be unfair to His creation. He created everything, and He alone has the right to treat His creation as He wills. He does not owe anyone anything as He is the One Who created them in the first place.

However, even though Allah has all the power and might and He can do whatever He wants, He does not treat His creation unfairly. He either treats them with His kindness and mercy and gives them more than they deserve, or He treats them with justice.

We must submit ourselves to Allah's will and decree. Human beings are short-sighted, and only know the immediate benefit of things. They do not know what is better for them in the long run—in this life or in the next life.

On the Day of Judgement, Allah will explain everything to us. On that day we will understand the wisdom behind Allah's decree and the reason for our suffering in this world. When everything will be explained to us, then we will come to understand it. On that day, we will be thankful to Allah and we will realise how merciful and kind He really is.

The tests that we face in our life is a sign that Allah loves us. Going through difficulties does not mean that we are bad. This is because when we pass the test, we achieve the higher grades of Paradise (Jannah) and we get closer to Allah. When we go through a difficult test, Allah forgives our sins. Sometimes when we are not doing a lot of good deeds, Allah will give us a test to help us become better. So, we should accept the tests that Allah gives us and try our best to pass them. If we do, then we will achieve Allah's love and be closer to Him.

Story: Prophet Musa عليه السلام and Khidr عليه السلام

The following story tells us how Allah knows what is better for us and how Allah helps us even though we think we are going through difficult times.

One day, Prophet Musa عليه السلام set out on a journey to meet Khidr عليه السلام. Khidr عليه السلام was a great servant of Allah who had special knowledge. When Prophet Musa عليه السلام met Khidr, he asked, "Can I stay with you so that you may teach me some of your knowledge?"

"You will not be able to have patience with me," Khidr عليه السلام replied.

However, Prophet Musa عليه السلام insisted and promised not to say anything, so Khidr عليه السلام agreed.

They both set out on the journey. They came to a boat and got onto it. Khidr عليه السلام made a hole in the boat and this made Prophet Musa عليه السلام angry. "Have you made a hole in the boat to drown the people on board?" he said.

However, Khidr عليه السلام simply replied, "Did I not tell you that you would not be able bear with me patiently?"

Prophet Musa عليه السلام asked Khidr عليه السلام for forgiveness and promised that he would not say anything again. So, they both went on their way till they met a boy. Khidr عليه السلام took the boy to the side and killed him. Prophet Musa عليه السلام was shocked by this. "Have you killed a harmless soul. This is a horrible thing!" Prophet Musa عليه السلام said.

But again, Khidr عليه السلام replied, "Did I not tell you that you would not be able bear with me patiently?"

Prophet Musa عليه السلام asked Khidr عليه السلام for forgiveness again and promised if he said something once more then he would leave. So Khidr agreed.

They both continued on their journey until they reached a town. They asked the townspeople for food, but they refused. Then they found a wall there, which was about to fall. Khidr عليه السلام started fixing the wall putting it straight. However, Prophet Musa عليه السلام was not pleased. He said, "If you wanted, you could have got paid for this."

"Now this is the time for us to go on our separate ways," Khidr عليه السلام said to Prophet Musa عليه السلام.

Khidr عليه السلام then started to explain everything to him. He said, "As for the boat, it belongs to some poor sailors. The cruel king was standing ahead of them to take away every undamaged boat by force. So, I made a hole in it to save it for them."

"As for the boy, his parents are believers. I feared that if he lives, he would become a disbeliever and he would hurt his parents. Allah will replace him with another child who will be better than him."

"And as for the wall, it belongs to two orphan boys. There is a treasure buried beneath and their father was a pious man. So, Allah wants them to grow bigger so that when they become adults they can dig out the treasure for themselves by the mercy of their Lord."

"I did not do this by my own choice (i.e. I did this by Allah's orders). This is the truth of the matter about which you could not stay patient."

Lesson 13

Other Types of Salah (Part 2)

We have been through some of the types of prayers (Salah) that are important for us to learn about. Let us continue learning about some more.

4. Extra Voluntary Prayers (Nawafil)

Allah has made the five daily prayers obligatory on every Muslim man and woman. However, there are also other prayers that are **voluntary (Nafl)**, and we should try to perform them daily to get extra reward from Allah and to attain high stations in Paradise (Jannah).

These prayers are offered at different times throughout the day. They cannot be offered at the times that are **disliked (Makruh)** (i.e. at sunrise, noon and sunset).

These voluntary prayers are:

i. The Tahajjud Prayer

This is the night prayer, which is performed in the last one-third of the night before dawn. It is performed after the `Isha prayer and before the Fajr prayer. For this prayer, a person wakes up in the darkness of the night and performs two-unit voluntary prayers. Two units is the minimum amount and twelve units is the maximum amount. The Sunnah is to perform eight units of prayer.

ii. The Ishraq Prayer

This is the prayer performed after sunrise and it must be at least twenty minutes after sunrise to perform this prayer. For this prayer, a person performs two-unit voluntary prayers. Two units is the minimum amount and six units is the maximum amount.

iii. The Duha Prayer

This is the mid-morning prayer when the sun has risen well above the horizon. The best time for this prayer is when the sun is midway between sunrise and noon. For this prayer, a person performs two-unit voluntary prayers. Two units is the minimum amount and twelve units is the maximum amount.

iv. The Awwabin Prayer

This prayer is performed between the Maghrib and `Isha' prayers. For this prayer, a person can perform either two long units of voluntary prayer or six short units.

5. The Tahiyyat al-Wudu' and Tahiyyat al-Masjid Prayers

The Tahiyyat al-Wudu' Prayer is performed straight after performing the Wudu' (the Ritual Ablution). This is a voluntary prayer and it consists of two units of prayer.

The Tahiyyat al-Masjid Prayer should be performed upon entering the mosque before sitting down. This is a voluntary prayer and it consists of two units of prayer. It is performed to greet the mosque and to show respect to it.

In both prayers, it is recommended to recite Surat al-Kafirun in the first unit and Surat al-Ikhlas in the second. You must make sure that both prayers are not performed at the disliked (Makruh) timings of prayer.

6. The Solar and Lunar Eclipse Prayers

The eclipse is a sign of Allah's power and greatness. During the solar eclipse, we perform two units of Sunnahh prayer known as the 'Solar Eclipse Prayer' (Salat al-Kusuf). This prayer can be performed in our homes individually or in the mosque in congregation. There is no Adhan or Iqama for this prayer. During this prayer, we lengthen the standing position and we lengthen the bowing and prostration positions.

The Lunar Eclipse Prayer (Salat al-Khusuf) should only be performed at home and not in congregation.

It is performed the same way as the Solar Eclipse Prayer (Salat al-Kusuf).

Performing two or four units of Sunnahh prayer is recommended at certain times of fear, such as during earthquakes, intense wind, thunderstorm or overwhelming darkness. This is because during times of fear, we should return to Allah, ask forgiveness for our sins and remember Him.

7. The Tarawih Prayer

During the month of Ramadan, we perform the Tarawih prayer in the night. It is usually performed between the four Fard of the `Isha' prayer and the Witr (Wajib) prayer.

The Tarawih prayer is **twenty units** in total and it is usually performed as ten sets of two units. After every four units, there is a short break known as a '**tarwihah**'.

The Tarawih prayer is performed by men in congregation, and it is recommended to recite the whole Qur'an throughout the month of Ramadan during this prayer. Women usually perform this prayer at home, but they can also perform it in the mosque with their family. If this prayer is missed, there is no Qada' prayer to make up for it.

At the end of every four units, during the short break (tarwihah), the following glorification is commonly recited in the mosques:

سُبْحَانَ ذِي الْمُلْكِ وَالْمَلَكُوْتِ. سُبْحَانَ ذِي الْعِزَّةِ وَالْعَظْمَةِ
وَالْهَيْبَةِ وَالْقُدْرَةِ وَالْكِبْرِيَاءِ وَالْجَبَرُوْتِ. سُبْحَانَ الْمَلِكِ الْحَيِّ
الَّذِيْ لَا يَنَامُ وَلَا يَمُوْتُ سُبُّوْحٌ قُدُّوْسٌ رَبُّنَا وَرَبُّ الْمَلَائِكَةِ
وَالرُّوْحِ. اَللّٰهُمَّ أَجِرْنَا مِنَ النَّارِ يَا مُجِيْرُ يَا مُجِيْرُ يَا مُجِيْرُ

Exalted is the Possessor of the Hidden and the Manifest Dominion. Exalted is the Possessor of Might, Greatness, Reverence, Power, Pride, and Majesty. Exalted is the Master, the Living, the One Who neither sleeps nor dies. All-Perfect, All-Holy, Our Lord, and the Lord of the Angels and the Holy Spirit (Angel Jibra'il). O Allah grant us refuge from the Hellfire. O Granter of refuge, O Granter of refuge, O Granter of refuge.

It is not obligatory to recite this glorification, because we can either recite it or just remain silent. It is also permissible to recite something else instead.

8. The Istikharah Prayer

The Istikharah Prayer is a special prayer which we perform to ask Allah for the best outcome in our decisions. It is a two-unit prayer in which it is recommended to recite Surat al-Kafirun in the first unit and Surat al-Ikhlas in the second unit. After the prayer, the following supplication (du`a) should be recited:

اَللّٰهُمَّ إِنِّيْ أَسْتَخِيْرُكَ بِعِلْمِكَ وَأَسْتَقْدِرُكَ بِقُدْرَتِكَ وَأَسْأَلُكَ مِنْ فَضْلِكَ الْعَظِيْمِ، فَإِنَّكَ تَقْدِرُ وَلَا أَقْدِرُ وَتَعْلَمُ وَلَا أَعْلَمُ وَأَنْتَ عَلَّامُ الْغُيُوْبِ. اَللّٰهُمَّ إِنْ كُنْتَ تَعْلَمُ أَنَّ هٰذَا الْأَمْرَ (*) خَيْرٌ لِيْ فِيْ دِيْنِيْ وَمَعَاشِيْ وَمَعَادِيْ وَعَاقِبَةِ أَمْرِيْ، فَاقْدُرْهُ وَيَسِّرْهُ لِيْ، ثُمَّ بَارِكْ لِيْ فِيْهِ. اَللّٰهُمَّ وَإِنْ كُنْتَ تَعْلَمُ أَنَّ هٰذَا الْأَمْرَ (*) شَرٌّ لِّيْ، فِيْ دِيْنِيْ وَمَعَاشِيْ وَمَعَادِيْ وَعَاقِبَةِ أَمْرِيْ، فَاصْرِفْهُ عَنِّيْ وَاصْرِفْنِيْ عَنْهُ، وَاقْدُرْ لِيَ الْخَيْرَ حَيْثُ كَانَ، ثُمَّ أَرْضِنِيْ بِهِ

O Allah! I seek goodness from Your Knowledge; I seek strength from Your Power (and Might); I ask You for Your Great Blessings; because You have the Power and I do not have power; You know everything, and I do not know; You have knowledge of the unseen. O Allah! If in Your Knowledge this matter [*the issue or matter should be mentioned here] is good for me, for my faith, my life, my death, and my hereafter then make it destined for me so that it takes effect with ease and then add blessings in it for me. O Allah! In Your Knowledge if this matter [*the issue or matter should be mentioned here] is bad for me, for my faith, my life, my death, and my hereafter then turn it away from me and turn me away from it. Destine for me whatever is better for me, and then make me satisfied with it:

This supplication should be made after the prayer for seven consecutive days. After seven days of praying, the person should do what feels right in their heart. It is not necessary that a dream is shown, or a sign is given.

The purpose of the Istikharah Prayer is to ask Allah for goodness in your decision. So, once the decision is made, the person should rely on Allah and put their full trust in Him.

9. The Tasbih Prayer

The Tasbih Prayer is a special prayer in which we recite the tasbih (glorification of Allah) **300 times**. It is reported that Ibn `Abbas was taught this prayer by the Prophet ﷺ (Ibn Majah).

This is an important prayer for the forgiveness of sins, and it should be performed at least once in a lifetime, if not every day, week, month or year.

The tasbih (glorification of Allah) that is recited in this prayer is:

سُبْحَانَ اللّٰهِ وَالْحَمْدُ لِلّٰهِ
وَلَا إِلٰهَ إِلَّا اللّٰهُ وَاللّٰهُ أَكْبَرُ

Glory be to Allah. All praise be to Allah. There is no God but Allah. Allah is the greatest:

How to Perform the Tasbih Prayer

The Tasbih Prayer is a four-unit prayer, in which the tasbih (glorification of Allah) is recited 75 times in every unit, making it 300 times in the whole prayer. The prayer is performed like a normal Nafl prayer, except at different points in the prayer the tasbih (glorification of Allah) is recited a specific number of times.

The following table explains when the tasbih (glorification of Allah) needs to be recited.

When to be Recited	Number of Times
After the Thana' and before the recitation	15
After the recitation and before bowing	10
During the bowing position	10
After raising the head from the bowing position	10
During the first prostration	10
During the short sitting between the prostrations	10
During the second prostration	10
Total Number of Recitations in Every Unit	**75**

10. Prayer in Times of Need

Whenever we are in times of difficulty or need, we should return to Allah and ask Him for help. We can do this by performing two units of prayer and reciting Surat al-Kafirun in the first unit and Surat al-Ikhlas in the second. The prayer for need is known as **Salat al-Hajah**, but there are other occasions when we may perform the two units of voluntary prayer for a specific need.

Some of them can be the following:

- When fearing an enemy (Salat al-Khawf)
- Before setting off on a journey (Salat as-Safar)
- After doing a sin and asking Allah for forgiveness (Salat at-Tawbah)
- Praying to Allah for rain (Salat al-Istisqa')

Lesson 14

A Muslim's Duty to Prophet Muhammad ﷺ

Allah has given us four duties with regards to Prophet Muhammad ﷺ (al-A`raf 7:157). They are:

1. Believing in the Prophet ﷺ
2. Respecting the Prophet ﷺ
3. Supporting the Prophet ﷺ
4. Following the Prophet ﷺ

Examples of how these four duties should be fulfilled are found in the lives of the Prophet's Companions.

The First Duty: Believing in the Prophet ﷺ

We must first believe in Prophet Muhammad ﷺ. If we truly believe in the Prophet ﷺ, we must love him, because love for the Prophet ﷺ is **the perfection of faith (Iman)**. The Prophet ﷺ said, "None of you believe until I am more beloved to him than his parents, children and all people." (al-Bukhari and Muslim).

One day, Prophet Muhammad ﷺ was walking with `Umar bin al-Khattab. `Umar said, "O Messenger of Allah! By Allah! You are more beloved to me than everything except my own soul." The Prophet ﷺ replied, "By Allah! None of you will believe until I am more beloved to him than his own self." Hearing this, `Umar replied, "By Allah! You are now more beloved to me than my own self." The Prophet ﷺ said, "Now, `Umar (your faith is perfect)." (al-Bukhari)

The Second Duty: Respecting the Prophet ﷺ

Allah commands us to respect and revere Prophet Muhammad ﷺ. Allah forbids us from even raising our voice above the voice of the Prophet ﷺ (al-Hujurat 49:2). We must always be respectful to the Prophet ﷺ, and not to disrespect him even once in case all our good deeds are destroyed.

`Urwah bin Mas`ud was sent as an ambassador by the Quraysh to the Prophet ﷺ. When `Urwah returned, he told the Quraysh, "O people! By Allah, I have been to kings and to Caesar, Khosrau and Najashi, yet I have never seen any of them respected by their followers as much as Muhammad is respected by his Companions. By Allah, if he spat, the saliva would fall in the hand of one of them who would rub it on his face and skin. If he ordered them, they would carry out his order immediately. If he performed ablution, they would struggle with each other to take the water that was left over; and when they spoke, they would lower their voices and would not look at him eye to eye out of respect for him." (al-Bukhari)

Anas bin Malik mentions an incident in which the Companions showed great respect for the Prophet ﷺ. He said that once while the Prophet ﷺ was having his hair cut, the Companions walked around the Prophet ﷺ like they were performing Tawaf. The Companions were careful to catch every strand of hair as they did not want a single strand of hair to fall on the ground (Muslim).

The Third Duty: Supporting the Prophet ﷺ

Supporting the Prophet ﷺ means supporting his religion and teachings. The Companions supported the Prophet ﷺ with their lives, money and time. They always did their best to support him and help him spread his message. Some examples from the lives of the Companions are given as follows.

Abu Bakr as-Siddiq was the first Muslim to call people to Islam publicly during the life of the Prophet ﷺ. When he called the polytheists to Islam, they got angry with him. They beat him and left him badly injured with his face full of blood. His family came and carried him home; they were certain Abu Bakr would die from his injuries.

They sat on his bedside waiting for him to recover, but he did not wake up until the end of the day. When Abu Bakr woke up, he asked, "What happened to the Prophet?" He kept on repeating this question, until his mother said, "By Allah! I do not know about your friend." Abu Bakr, however, did not care about his pain and only asked, “What happened to the Prophet?” Someone told him that the Prophet ﷺ is fine and that he was in Dar al-Arqam (seminary).

Hearing this, Abu Bakr said, “By Allah, I will not have any food or drink unless I go to see Allah’s Messenger.” The Prophet ﷺ and his Companions came to see Abu Bakr. When the Prophet ﷺ met Abu Bakr, he kissed him on his forehead and felt sad for him. The Muslims also felt sad for him and began to hug him (Ibn Kathir in al-Bidaya wa an-Nihaya).

On another occasion, the Prophet ﷺ asked the Companions to give charity. `Umar said, “I have some money. Today I will give half of my wealth.” When `Umar handed over his wealth, the Prophet ﷺ asked him, “O `Umar, what have you left for your family?” “I have left them half of my wealth,” replied `Umar. Later, Abu Bakr came with all of his wealth and handed it over. “What have you left for your family,” asked the Prophet ﷺ. “I have left Allah and His Messenger for them,” replied Abu Bakr (at-Tirmidhi).

The Fourth Duty: Following the Prophet ﷺ

The Prophet ﷺ explained the importance of following him. He said, "Whoever obeys me, obeys Allah; and whoever disobeys me, disobeys Allah." (al-Bukhari) When we follow the Prophet ﷺ it is a sign that we love him; it is one of the ways to strengthen our love for him. This is because the relationship between love and action is like the relationship between the soul and the body.

The Companion `Abdullah bin `Umar used to copy every action of the Prophet ﷺ. He used to memorise everything he would hear from him. He would ask the senior Companions about the Prophet's sayings and actions and he would record them. He would follow the Prophet's footsteps to every mosque and offer his prayer there. He would choose those roads and streets on which the Prophet ﷺ used to travel. And every year he would perform the Hajj and stand in the place where the Prophet ﷺ used to stand (al-`Asqalani in al-Isaba fi Tamyiz as-Sahaba).

Lesson 15

The Companions

Prophet Muhammad ﷺ is the best of all creation and his Ummah is the best Ummah (Community). From his Ummah, the Companions are the greatest. No one can be equal to a single Companion of the Prophet ﷺ and respecting them is part of our faith.

A Companion is a Muslim man or woman who met the Prophet ﷺ and died as a Muslim. The word '**Sahabah**' is the Arabic term for Companions. A male Companion is called a '**Sahabi**' and a female Companion is called a '**Sahabiyyah**'. There were thousands of Companions of the Prophet ﷺ; according to one view, there were about 124,000 companions.

The Excellence and Virtues of the Companions

The Prophet ﷺ spoke about the excellence and virtues of his Companions. He commanded us to follow them and to walk in their footsteps. In one hadith, he said, "The similarity of my Companions is like the similarity of the stars by which one is guided. So, whichever one of my Companions you follow, you will be guided." (`Abd bin Humayd)

The Prophet ﷺ warned his Ummah from belittling or speaking harshly of any of his Companions. He said, "Do not insult my Companions. By Him in whose hand my soul is, if one of you donated the amount of gold equal to Mount Uhud, it would not equal to as much as one cup donated by one of them, or (even) half of it." (al-Bukhari and Muslim)

Speaking of the miracles of the Companions and their blessings, Abu Sa`id al-Khudri narrates that the Prophet ﷺ said, "A time will come when a group of people will defend Islam against the enemy, and it will be said, 'Is there any Companion of the Prophet among you?' They will say, 'Yes.' And, so (through the means of that Companion) victory will be given to them (by Allah)."

"Then a time will come when a group of people will defend Islam, and it will be said, 'Is there anyone among you who has been with a Companion of the Prophet?' They will say, 'Yes.' And, so (through the means of that person) victory will be given to them (by Allah)."

"Then a time will come when a group of people will defend Islam, and it will be said, 'Is there anyone among you who has been with someone who has been in the company of a Companion of the Prophet?' They will say, 'Yes.' And, so (through the means of that person) victory will be given to them (by Allah)." (al-Bukhari and Muslim)

The Rightly Guided Caliphs

Among the Companions, there are many respected personalities. The first and the most important of these are the **'Rightly Guided Caliphs' (al-Khulafa' ar-Rashidin al-Mahdiyyin)**. The Rightly Guided Caliphs were the political successors of Prophet Muhammad ﷺ. They became the leaders of the Ummah after the Prophet ﷺ passed from this world.

There were **four** Rightly Guided Caliphs, and they were (in order of their succession):

1st Caliph: Abu Bakr as-Siddiq	2nd Caliph: `Umar bin al-Khattab
3rd Caliph: `Uthman bin `Affan	4th Caliph: 'Ali bin Abi Talib

We must follow the way of the Rightly Guided Caliphs. Al-Irbad bin Sariyah relates that one day the Prophet ﷺ stood up to deliver a speech and he said such words that made everyone tearful. The Companions asked the Prophet ﷺ for advice. So, the Prophet ﷺ said, "Follow my Sunna and the Sunna of the Rightly Guided Caliphs (after me) and clench it firmly with your teeth (i.e. hold fast to it)." (Ibn Majah)

The Prophet ﷺ praised the unique qualities of each of the Rightly Guided Caliphs. In one hadith, Anas bin Malik relates that the Prophet ﷺ said, "The most merciful of my Ummah towards my Ummah is Abu Bakr. The one who follows the religion of Allah most strictly is `Umar. The sincerest of them in shyness and modesty is `Uthman. (And) the best judge is `Ali bin Abi Talib." (Ibn Majah)

The Rightly Guided Caliphs were the greatest Companions and they were the best people in the Ummah. Muhammad bin al-Hanafiyya, who is the son of the fourth Rightly Guided Caliph, `Ali, asked his father, "Who is the best person after the Prophet?" His father, `Ali, replied, "Abu Bakr." "Then who?" asked Muhammad bin al-Hanafiyya. "Then it is `Umar," `Ali replied. Muhammad bin al-Hanafiyya said that he feared his father would say `Uthman next (because he wanted his father to name himself), so he asked, 'Is it you next?', but `Ali replied, "I am just a (humble) member of the Muslim community." (al-Bukhari)

Mentioning the virtues of the Rightly Guided Caliphs, Anas bin Malik relates that the Prophet ﷺ once climbed Mount Uhud, with Abu Bakr, `Umar and `Uthman. Mount Uhud trembled out of respect for them. The Prophet ﷺ said, "Be firm, O Uhud. For on you are a Prophet, a Siddiq (a Verifier of Truth) and two martyrs." (al-Bukhari)

The Ten Promised Paradise

Other than the four 'Rightly Guided Caliphs', there are other respected personalities among the Companions. There are ten Companions who were promised Paradise, and they are known as **'al-`Asharah al-Mubashsharah'**.

Mentioning the names of these ten companions, `Abd al-Rahman bin `Awf narrates that the Prophet ﷺ said, "Abu Bakr will go to Paradise. `Umar will go to Paradise. `Uthman will go to Paradise. `Ali will go to Paradise. Talhah will go to Paradise. Al-Zubayr will go to Paradise. `Abd al-Rahman bin `Awf will go to Paradise. Sa`d bin Abi Waqqas will go to Paradise. Sa`id will go to Paradise. And Abu `Ubaydah bin al-Jarrah will go to Paradise." (at-Tirmidhi)

Other Great Companions

Among the Companions, the Rightly Guided Caliphs are the greatest in their ranking and status. They have been given superiority over all other Companions. The next in order of ranking are the ten who were promised Paradise, and then the 313 who fought in the Battle of Badr.

The **313 Companions** who fought in the Battle of Badr were among the sincerest and most loyal followers of the Prophet ﷺ. Among them were Abu Bakr, `Umar, `Uthman and `Ali. Speaking of their virtue, `Ali relates the glad tidings given to them by Allah. He narrates that the Prophet ﷺ said, "Allah turned to the veterans of Badr and said, 'You can do whatever you want for I have made Paradise compulsory for you.'" (Bukhari and Muslim)

After these 313 Companions, the Companions who are next in order are the 1400 (male and female

Companions) who pledged their allegiance to the Prophet ﷺ under the tree at Hudaybiyah. Allah praised these 1400 Companions in the Qur'an (al-Fath 48:18), and they came to be known as '**Ashab ash-Shajarah' (the People of the Tree)**.

Lesson 16

The Ahl al-Bayt

The Ahl al-Bayt are the blessed family of the Prophet ﷺ. The family of the Prophet ﷺ include his blessed wives, his pure daughters, his cousin `Ali and his grandsons al-Hasan and al-Husayn.

The Excellence and Virtues of the Ahl al-Bayt

Like the Companions, the Ahl al-Bayt are also a source of guidance for the Ummah. Zayd bin Arqam reports that the Prophet ﷺ was delivering a sermon one day between Makkah and Madinah. In this sermon, he praised Allah and said, "I am leaving behind you two weighty things. The first of them is the **Book of Allah (the Qur'an)**… (and the second of them is) the **people of my household**. I remind you of my family. I remind you of my family. I remind you of my family." (Muslim)

In another hadith, according to Jabir bin `Abd Allah, the Prophet ﷺ said, "O people! I am leaving behind something if you follow them, you will never be led astray: **The Book of Allah** and **my household**." (at-Tirmidhi)

Just as it is necessary to respect the Companions of the Prophet ﷺ and to speak well of them, we must also respect the holy family of the Prophet ﷺ. In fact, it is necessary to love them and honour them without any exception. Ibn `Abbas relates that the Prophet ﷺ said, "Love me for the sake of Allah's love and love my family for the sake of my love." (at-Tirmidhi)

In another hadith, al-Abbas relates that the Prophet ﷺ said, “Faith (Iman) will not enter the heart of a man until he loves my family for the sake of Allah and for my sake (due to my family relation with them).” (Ibn Majah and al-Hakim) Similarly, Abu Hurayrah reports that the Prophet ﷺ said, “The best of you is the one who is the best to my family after me.” (al-Hakim)

According to Abu Layla, the Prophet ﷺ said, “A person does not believe until I become more beloved to him than himself, my family is more beloved to him than his own family, and my relatives are more beloved to him than his own relatives.” (at-Tabarani)

Abu Sa`id reports that the Prophet ﷺ warned, “By the One in Whose hand is my soul, no man hates

us – i.e. the people of my household — except Allah will enter him into the Hellfire." (Ibn Hibban and al-Hakim)

The Five Purified Ones

The family of the Prophet's youngest daughter, Sayyida Fatimah al-Zahra', have a special status among the Prophet's relatives. They are the spiritual successors of the Prophet ﷺ and the leaders of the Prophet's Ummah on the Day of Judgement. To mark their uniqueness and excellent status, they have been given the title of the '**Five Purified Ones**'. This title has been derived from the authentic hadith.

The holy personalities who belong to the 'Five Purified Ones' are:

1. Prophet Muhammad ﷺ

2. His cousin and son-in-law, Sayyiduna `Ali al-Murtada (who is also the fourth Rightly Guided Caliph)

3. His youngest daughter, Sayyidah Fatimah az-Zahra' (she was the wife of `Ali al-Murtada)

4. His elder grandson, Imam al-Hasan

5. His younger grandson, Imam al-Husayn

Mother of the Believers `A'ishah reports that the Prophet ﷺ was wearing a striped cloak made from black camel hair. Imam al-Hasan came and the Prophet ﷺ wrapped him under it. Then came Imam al-Husayn and he wrapped him under it along with al-Hasan. Then came Fatimah az-Zahra'and he took her and wrapped her under it. Then came `Ali al-Murtada and he also took him under it, and then he recited the verse: "*Allah only intends to remove all the impurity of sins from you, O Ahl al-Bayt, and make you absolutely pure and clean by blessing you with (perfect) purity.*" (al-Ahzab 33:33) (Muslim and al-Hakim)

`Umar bin Abi Salamah reports that the above verse (al-Ahzab 33:33) was revealed in the house of the Mother of the Believers Umm Salamah. She narrates that after the Prophet ﷺ covered al-Hasan, al-Husayn, Fatimah and `Ali, he prayed, "O Allah, this is my household (Ahl al-Bayt). Remove from them impurity and purify them perfectly." Umm Salamah asked the Prophet ﷺ if she could be among them, but the Prophet ﷺ replied, "You are in your place (i.e. as a Mother of the Believers) and you are upon goodness." (at-Tirmidhi)

Due to this incident, the 'Five Purified Ones' are also known as **'Ahl al-Kisa'' (The People of the Cloak)**.

The Mothers of the Believers

The Prophet's blessed wives have a special status among the Ummah and they are our mothers (al-Ahzab 33:6). Each of the pure wives of the Prophet ﷺ was given the honourable title of **'Mother of the Believers' (Umm al-Mu'minin)**.

The following twelve are the Mothers of the Believers:

1. Khadijah bint al-Khuwaylid: She is the first Muslim and the Prophet's first wife. Anas bin Malik relates that the Prophet ﷺ said, "The best women of the world are: Maryam, the daughter of `Imran; Khadija bint Khuwaylid; Fatimah, the Prophet's daughter, and Asiya, the wife of Pharaoh." (at-Tirmidhi)

2. `A'ishahh bint Abi Bakr: She was the daughter of the first Rightly Guided Caliph, Abu Bakr. `Amr bin al-`As relates that he asked the Prophet ﷺ "Which person is the most beloved to you?" He replied, "`A'ishah." Then I asked, "What about from the men?" He said, "Her father (Abu Bakr)." Then I asked, "Then who?" He said, "`Umar."

(al-Bukhari and Muslim)

3. Sawdah bint Zam`ah
4. Hafsah bint `Umar bin al-Khattab
5. Zaynab bint Khuzaymah
6. Umm Salamah
7. Zaynab bint Jahsh
8. Juwayriyah bint al-Harith
9. Mariyah al-Qubtiyyah
10. Umm Habibah
11. Safiyyah bint Huyayy
12. Maymunah bint al-Harith

Lesson 17

Sawm (Fasting)

There are special times in the year when Muslims come together to worship Allah. One such time is the holy month of **Ramadan**. The month of Ramadan begins with the sighting of **the new crescent moon (Hilal)** at the end of the month of Sha`ban. Muslims all around the world fast during the daylight hours of this month as it is one of the five pillars of Islam.

During this holy month, we begin our day by waking up before dawn to take part in a blessed meal called '**Suhur**'. We fast throughout the day and do not eat or drink anything. When the sun sets, we break our fast (preferably with some dates and water). The act of breaking the fast is called '**Iftar**'.

After the Iftar, the men go to the mosque to join in the **Tarawih** prayer, while women offer this prayer at home. They perform twenty units of prayer and listen to the recitation of the whole Qur'an throughout the month.

In the last ten days of Ramadan, some people seclude themselves in the mosque (or for women in their home). They worship Allah through the nights in search of a special night called the 'Night of Power' (Laylat al-Qadr). This is known as '**I`tikaf**'.

The **Night of Power (Laylah al-Qadr)** is better than 1000 months, because worship on this one night is equal to 1000 months of worship. This special night is in the last ten days of Ramadan, and more specifically it is on one of the **odd nights** (i.e., the 21st, 23rd, 25th, 27th or 29th of Ramadan). On this night, Allah forgives people all of their sins and the angels of mercy come down.

The Rules of Fasting

The basic rule of fasting is not to eat or drink anything during daylight hours, with an intention to keep the fast. It begins at **dawn**, when the first rays of sunlight can be seen on the horizon (the same time when the Fajr prayer begins) and it ends at **sunset**.

There are different types of fasts. Some of them are:

1. OBLIGATORY (FARD) FASTS

Examples of the obligatory (Fard) fasts are the ones in the **month of Ramadan**, both the **Ada'** (the ones performed on time) and the **Qada'** (the ones made up afterwards).

2. RECOMMENDED (SUNNAH) FASTS

Examples of the recommended (Sunnah) fasts are the fast of **`Ashura'** on the 9th and 10th of Muharram, fasting on **Mondays** and **Thursdays**, the **six days in Shawwal** and the **13th, 14th and 15th of every lunar month**.

3. DISLIKED (MAKRUH) FASTS

Examples of the disliked (Makruh) fasts are the **10th of Muharram on its own** or **singling out Friday** as a day for fasting.

4. IMPERMISSIBLE (HARAM) FASTS

Examples of the impermissible (Haram) fasts are the fast on the **two days of `Id** and the **11$^{th}$, 12$^{th}$ and 13$^{th}$ of Dhu al-Hijjah** (the three days after `Id al-Adha).

Other than these five days, it is **permissible (Mubah)** to fast on any other day of the year. Fasting on a day that is NOT obligatory or recommended would be counted as a **voluntary (Nafl)** fast.

Like the prayer (Salah), it is **obligatory (Fard)** to have an intention for the fast. The **intention (niyyah)** is simply to make up your mind that you will be fasting for the day. It should be made before the fast begins, from any time after sunset from the night before. For example, if you are making up a missed fast from Ramadan (Qada'), it is necessary to specify it in the intention the night before.

For the fast in the month of Ramadan, you just need to have an intention to keep the fast. Even if you missed the Suhur (pre-dawn meal) and did not make an intention from the night before, you can keep the fast and make the intention in the morning at any time before midday. This also applies to the voluntary (Nafl) fast.

When we are fasting, the following actions BREAK the fast:

1. Eating and drinking intentionally or even by accident.
2. Inhaling smoke or fumes intentionally (such as from oud, a traditional Arabian incense).
3. Swallowing medicine.
4. Vomiting intentionally.

Doing the following actions does NOT break the fast:

1. Eating or drinking forgetfully.
2. Swallowing leftover food from between the teeth (if it is less than the size of a chickpea).
3. Something going down the throat not by one's own action.
4. Having a bath, cutting the hair or trimming the nails.
5. Putting in eye drops, applying cream on the skin or wearing make-up.
6. Vomiting or bleeding.
7. Brushing the teeth with toothpaste.

Doing the following actions during the fast is **disliked (Makruh)** and SHOULD be avoided:

1. Tasting food or drink without swallowing it.
2. Chewing something, such as a rubber or plastic. However, chewing bubble gum or a sweet will break the fast as it has sugar in it.
3. Gargling water in the mouth in such a way that it risks going down the throat.
4. Complaining about hunger or thirst.
5. Swallowing one's own saliva.
6. Arguing, fighting or using filthy words.
7. Backbiting, lying, swearing and doing other sinful acts.

Doing any of the above does NOT break the fast.

Spiritual Benefits of Fasting

The month of Ramadan is a great opportunity to bring positive changes in our life. It is a month when we break our normal patterns of behaviour to concentrate on our connection with Allah and getting closer to Him. The Qur'an explains that fasting has been given to us so that we can become pious and God-fearing.

Ramadan is a month-long period of training to help us get spiritually fit and close to Allah; it is a time when we look at how we live our life and we try to become a better human being.

In this blessed month, it becomes easier to avoid sin and to do good acts. If we can control ourselves from eating and drinking, it means we can also control our eyes, tongue, ears and hands from harming others and doing sin. While fasting, we must not swear or speak indecently, and if someone tries to fight with us, we should say, 'I am fasting.'

Fasting is not just about remaining hungry and thirsty all day; it is about bringing positive changes in our behaviour. Prophet Muhammad ﷺ explained that Allah has no need for the person who fasts but does not stop doing bad deeds (al-Bukhari). People who backbite, lie, swear, be rude and create trouble gain nothing from their fast other than remaining hungry or thirsty. We do not just fast with our stomach only; we fast with every part of our body which means we need to stay away from all bad actions.

When we fast, we should try to develop good qualities in our personality such as learning to share, being grateful to Allah and learning to live without certain things such as too much food and drink.

When we feel the pain of hunger in our belly we should remember the poor and think of ways in which we can help them; and when we break the fast we should think of ways that we can share the blessings that Allah has given to us. Doing this will help us to become thankful to Allah and make us want less of this world. The person who does all this achieves the fruits of Ramadan and he or she fasts for the sake of Allah.

Medical Benefits of Fasting

It is important to give the body a rest. Eating all day and eating too much is not good for our health. Just like it is important to eat the right types of food, it is also important to give our bodies a break from eating as well. Working the body non-stop without a break brings it a lot of harm and damage, leading to health problems later in life. A good way of giving the body a break is by fasting.

Fasting is one of the best methods to regulate (control) our body and to keep everything working as normal. When we eat more than we need, the extra food remains in the body. It gets stored as fat or stays in the bloodstream as sugar, and it remains there until it gets used up. When we fast, we give the body a chance to use that leftover fat and sugar, and this helps the body to return to its normal working condition.

Fasting gives the body a chance to take care of itself. Instead of breaking down food into fat and sugar, the body gets a chance to repair its cells and to get rid of its rubbish. Therefore, the body heals and returns to its best condition; the brain works faster, and when a person eats, he or she feels satisfied quicker.

When we break the fast, it is important to eat the right kind of food. We can destroy the positive effects of fasting by eating oily food or junk food. When breaking the fast, drink plenty of water and eat fresh fruit and vegetables. This will provide the body with the fuel it needs to stay healthy and active. Eat enough to get rid of your hunger but do not overeat. Doing this will help you to look after your body and Allah will reward you and count you among His grateful servants.

Lesson 18

Pen Portrait of Prophet Muhammad ﷺ

Have you ever wondered what the greatest, most perfect and the most beautiful human being looked like?

Have you ever thought about what it was that the Companions actually saw when they looked at the blessed person of Prophet Muhammad ﷺ?

Prophet Muhammad ﷺ is the greatest and most beautiful human being Allah ever created.

Everyone who ever saw him was fascinated by his unique physical beauty, beautiful character and noble personality. The Companion 'Ali would often say, "No one ever saw anyone like the Prophet ﷺ, before him or after him."

The love and attachment that the Companions had with the Prophet ﷺ was so great that all of them, recorded and reported every tiny detail of the Prophet's blessed life.

Not only his teachings and practices, they also recorded in a lot of detail how the Prophet ﷺ looked, his personal habits and how he behaved in every situation.

Let us now look at some of the loving and beautiful descriptions that the Companions left for us, so that we may learn about the Prophet's beauty. By doing this, we can know him better and recognise and love him ﷺ.

His Holy Face

The Prophet's blessed face shone like the moon. Some descriptions of his blessed face are detailed as following:

- His skin was a radiant white, tinted with a rosy redness.
- His blessed eyes were black, deep and widely set. The eyeballs were very dark, the whiteness was bright white, with a little bit of pink at the ends.

- He had long eyelashes that naturally curled at the ends.
- His eyebrows were long and arched like bows, and did not connect, although it looked like they did.
- He had a wide forehead.
- His blessed nose was distinctive, raised and shining.
- His blessed beard was thick.
- His teeth were well set, separated, evenly spaced and shined like pearls.
- He had smooth cheeks and a wide mouth.

His Blessed Hair

The Prophet's blessed hair were not too curly and not too straight. His hair was thick and wavy.

He had three different lengths for his hair:

1. Up to his blessed earlobes.
2. Between his ears and shoulders.
3. Long, down to his blessed shoulders.

His Blessed Figure

The following are some descriptions of the Prophet's blessed figure (body):

- The Prophet ﷺ was neither too tall, nor short. He was of an average height and a medium build. However, when a very tall person walked with him, he appeared to be taller.
- His shoulders were wide, chest was strong, and he had large bones and joints.
- His chest and stomach were balanced.
- His arms were long and powerful.
- His hands, palms and the soles of his blessed feet were all thick.

- His fingers were long, with an even fair skin tone and smooth skin.
- His neck was balanced, toned and elegant.
- His legs were powerful, forceful and firm.
- The soles of his blessed feet were deep and hollow. The skin of his blessed feet was so smooth that even water would not stick to them.

His Blessed Walk

The Prophet ﷺ walked with purpose and firmness, in a strong way and at the same time with gentleness and easiness.

He lifted his legs with power, leaning forward a little, as if coming down from a higher to a lower level.

His movements were made with ease and he walked very fast without appearing to rush. The Companions found it difficult to keep up with him, even when he was walking at an apparently normal pace.

He did not drag his blessed feet on the ground nor let his body sag from side to side.

The Seal of Prophecy (Khatam an-Nubuwwah)

One of the most amazing physical features of Prophet Muhammad ﷺ was a divine sign of the finality of his Prophethood, which was on his back, between his shoulder blades.

As this sign was not like anything else in the world, the Companions could not describe the exact details. However, those who were fortunate enough to see it, described it the way they saw it.

It is described as a raised part of the skin between his blessed shoulder blades, equal to the size of a pigeon's egg. It was surrounded by some small hairs and beauty marks.

Lesson 19

Rightly Guided Caliphs – Abu Bakr and `Umar

The First Rightly Guided Caliph: Abu Bakr as-Siddiq

His real name is `Abd Allah bin Abi Quhafa. Abu Bakr was his nickname. He was the first man to enter Islam. He was given the title '**as-Siddiq**' (the Verifier of Truth) because at a time when many people did not believe the Prophet ﷺ after his Night Journey to Jerusalem, Abu Bakr stood by his side and declared his faith in the Prophet's truthfulness.

His Virtues and Excellence

Some of the virtues of Abu Bakr as-Siddiq are related below:

- Ibn `Abbas relates that the Prophet ﷺ said, "If I were to take a close friend (Khalil) from my Ummah, it would have been Abu Bakr. However, he is my brother and Companion." (al-Bukhari and Muslim)

- `A'isha as-Siddiqa narrates that the Prophet ﷺ said, "It is not befitting for a people if Abu Bakr is among them and someone other than him leads them." (at-Tirmidhi)

- Ibn `Umar reports that the Prophet ﷺ said to Abu Bakr, "You are my Companion at the Kawthar and my Companion in the cave." (at-Tirmidhi)

- Abu Hurayra relates that the Prophet ﷺ said, "There is no one who has done any favour on us except that we have repaid him for it — all except Abu Bakr, for his favour will only be repaid to him by Allah on the Day of Judgement." (at-Tirmidhi)

Moments from His Life

The life of Abu Bakr as-Siddiq is full of service and devotion to the Prophet ﷺ. One of the greatest moments in his life was when he accompanied the Prophet ﷺ on his journey to Madinah.

It is mentioned that when they arrived at Cave Thawr, Abu Bakr said to the Prophet ﷺ, "Let me enter the cave before you so I can see if there is anything harmful in there such as a snake." So, Abu Bakr entered the cave and started to search with his hand to find any snake holes. Every time he found a hole he would tear a piece off his shirt and plug it in the hole. He kept on doing this until he tore up all of his shirt. However, one hole was still not covered, so he placed the heel of his foot on its entrance to cover it.

After requesting the Prophet ﷺ to enter the cave, the Prophet ﷺ asked, "O Abu Bakr, where is your shirt?" Abu Bakr told him about what he did, and the Prophet ﷺ raised his hands in prayer and said, "O Allah! Make Abu Bakr with me on the Day of Judgement." Allah revealed to the Prophet ﷺ that he had accepted his supplication. (Abu Nu`aym)

Anas relates that when Abu Bakr was in the cave with the Prophet ﷺ he said to him about the disbelievers who were searching for them, "If they look to their feet, they will see us." But the Prophet ﷺ replied, "What do you think, O Abu Bakr, about the two, for whom Allah is the third (among them)?" (al-Bukhari and Muslim)

On another occasion, the Prophet ﷺ asked the Companions to donate money to the cause of Islam. So, all the Companions donated whatever they could. `Umar bin al-Khattab had a lot of wealth at that time. He knew that from all the Companions, Abu Bakr always donated the most. So, he saw this as an opportunity to give more than him.

`Umar gathered all his wealth and divided it into two. Half of it he would keep and the other half he would give as charity. He then went to the Prophet ﷺ with half of his total wealth. When the Prophet ﷺ saw that `Umar had brought a lot of valuables, he asked him, "What have you left for your family?" "I have left them the same amount," replied `Umar.

Then Abu Bakr came. He had donated everything that he had. When the Prophet ﷺ saw this, he asked, "O Abu Bakr, what have you left for your family?" Abu Bakr replied, "I have left them Allah and His

Messenger." Seeing that Abu Bakr had donated everything and had not left anything behind for himself and his family, `Umar said to himself, "I will never do better than him in anything." (at-Tirmidhi and Abu Dawud)

Then Angel Jibra'il came to the Prophet ﷺ and gave Allah's greeting to him and said, "Allah wants you to ask Abu Bakr: 'Are you pleased with Me in this state of poverty or displeased?'" So, the Prophet ﷺ said, "O Abu Bakr! Allah sends His greetings of peace to you and asks, 'Are you pleased with Me in this state of poverty or displeased?'" "Displeased with my Lord?" Abu Bakr exclaimed, "I am pleased with my Lord! I am pleased with my Lord! I am pleased with my Lord!" (Abu Nu`aym)

The Second Caliph: `Umar al-Faruq

His name is `Umar bin al-Khattab. He was given the title '**al-Faruq**' (the Distinguisher between Truth and Falsehood) because after his conversion to Islam, the Muslims received a great boost and were able to announce their faith openly in Makkah. `Umar al-Faruq was the most just and fair, and his rule was one of the greatest and most remarkable periods of human history. He was the first person to have the title **'Commander of the Faithful' (Amir al-Mu'minin)**.

His Virtues and Excellence

Some of the virtues of `Umar al-Faruq are related below:

- `Umar was so strong in his devotion to Islam that even Shaytan was afraid of him. The Prophet ﷺ once said to `Umar, "I swear by Him in Whose Hand is my soul, Shaytan would never want to walk next to you on a pathway, except that he would take a pathway different from yours." (al-Bukhari and Muslim)

- Ibn `Umar narrates that the Prophet ﷺ said, "Allah has placed the truth on the tongue and heart of `Umar." (at-Tirmidhi and Abu Dawud)

- `A'isha reports that the Prophet ﷺ used to say, "There were people in the former nations who would be inspired (i.e. the angels would speak through them). If there was such a person in my Ummah, then `Umar bin al-Khattab would be one of them." (Muslim and at-Tirmidhi)

Moments from His Life

There were many inspirational moments from the life of `Umar bin al-Khattab. Some of them are related below.

During his leadership, `Umar bin al-Khattab was delivering a talk while some of the Muslims were fighting the enemy forces in a distant land. In the middle of the sermon, he raised his voice and shouted, "O Sariya, take cover by the mountain!" Later, after the battle, Sariya sent a message to `Umar, saying, "O Commander of the Faithful, we were suddenly trapped by our enemy, and they were about to defeat us when we heard a voice telling us to take cover by the mountain. So, we put our backs to the mountain and by the grace of Allah we were able to defeat them." (Ahmad bin Hanbal)

Under the leadership of `Umar bin al-Khattab, Islam had spread far and wide from Egypt to Iran and from North Africa to Armenia. `Umar bin al-Khattab was the most powerful leader at that time, but even though he had all the power and wealth, he chose to lead a simple lifestyle. He would guard the streets of Madinah at night on foot and he made sure everyone was doing well and receiving their rights.

One night, as he was guarding the streets of Madinah, he heard small children in a house crying. `Umar bin al-Khattab went to the house and asked the mother why her children were crying. She told him that she did not have any food. Hearing about the woman's difficult situation, `Umar bin al-Khattab went straight to the Bayt al-Mal (State Treasury) and gathered together some food and put them in a sack. He then carried the food on his back. His servant asked to carry it for him, but `Umar replied, "No, it is my burden to carry. You will not carry my burden for me on the Day of Judgment." After carrying the food to the poor woman's home, `Umar then started cooking the food and preparing it for the children. Once it was prepared, he fed the hungry children with his own hands, and played with them until they fell happily asleep.

Another famous example that shows his humility and sincerity was when he travelled to Jerusalem to accept the keys to the city. On his way to the city, he travelled in a simple manner with one assistant and one camel. Throughout the journey, he would take turns with his assistant to ride on the camel. As they entered Jerusalem, the people of the city saw that the Rightly Guided Caliph was holding the camel's leash and his assistant was riding the camel.

The clothes worn by `Umar bin al-Khattab were patched because they had been mended. So, one of the Muslims suggested that he change his clothes because the people of Jerusalem were used to seeing the magnificent clothes of the kings. `Umar bin al-Khattab became angry by this and told him that Allah gave them honour when they had been a disgraced nation, and that honour is only achieved by acting upon the teachings given by Allah and His Messenger.

After receiving the keys of the city, the Rightly Guided Caliph `Umar allowed the Christians and Jews to continue living as they did previously and to practice their religion with freedom. He made sure that no church was converted into a mosque. Seeing the simplicity of the Caliph, his humility and Islam's good treatment towards non-Muslims, many Christians and Jews accepted Islam and became Muslims. The example of `Umar, the Rightly Guided Caliph, is a shining example for all times.

Lesson 20

Zakah and Sadaqah

Zakah (the poor due) is one of the five pillars of Islam, which is mentioned in the Qur'an many times together with the Salah. It is a financial worship in which a Muslim adult gives **2.5% (1/40)** of his or her savings to the poor and needy. It is not a governmental tax, but a religious duty and it is the right of the poor people over the wealth of the rich.

The meaning of the word 'Zakah' is **purity** and **growth**. It is given this name because when we give a small part of our wealth to the poor and needy Allah purifies our wealth and gives us more. Zakah does not lessen our wealth; it increases it because it brings blessings to it.

It is important to give the Zakah (the poor due) because it teaches us to purify our inner selves from greed, jealousy and stinginess. It also helps us to appreciate the things that Allah has given to us and to share them with others.

The Zakah (poor due) is a great way for a society to grow and become wealthy. For example, if water stays in a tank for a long time, it becomes mouldy and decays. If we want to keep the water clean and fresh, we need to keep it constantly flowing. Similarly, with money, a society remains wealthy when there is an easy flow of money between people and it is shared fairly. If money is held in one place, such as a big bank or in the hands of a few wealthy people, then it leads to less money in society and everyone becomes poorer.

Through the Zakah (the poor due), Allah orders the wealthy Muslims to give a small amount of their savings to the poor, so that the poor have money to spend on the things that they need. In this way, there is greater fairness in society, and the poor can live with respect and dignity leading society to prosper. Everyone in society is helped through the system of Zakah, and this leads to an increase in blessings for all.

The Rules of Zakah

The Zakah (poor due) is when Muslim adults give away 2.5% of their wealth to those people who are allowed to receive it.

The **Nisab** is the minimum amount of money a person must have for them to pay Zakah and they need to have the Nisab (minimum amount) for one lunar year. It is obligatory to pay the Zakah for those who have this amount of money saved after a lunar year passes.

The Nisab (minimum amount) is equal to 87 grams of gold or 612 grams of silver, or any amount of money that is equal to the lowest of these two in value. For example, if one gram of silver costs 41 pence, then you would need savings of £250 to reach the Nisab (41 pence x 612 grams of silver = £250. We must keep in mind that the Nisab rate changes every day).

If a Muslim, male or female, has the Nisab after one

lunar year, then the Zakah would become obligatory and they would have to pay it. The lunar year starts when a person has reached the Nisab amount. The Nisab is only the minimum amount to make the Zakah obligatory on a person.

The Zakah has to be paid on all savings. For example, if someone has saved one thousand pounds, then they will pay £25 as Zakah. (To calculate the Zakah, add up your saving and times it by 0.025, e.g. £1000 x 0.025 = £25, or divide it by 40, e.g. £1000 ÷ 40 = £25.)

The Zakah must be paid to the poor and needy, i.e. those people who have less than the Nisab amount. It can also be given to the homeless, a stranded traveller or a beggar.

When giving the Zakah, we must have an intention in our heart that this money is being given to them as Zakah. The Zakah cannot be given to build mosques, hospitals or schools. It must be given only to those people who are eligible.

The Sadaqat al-Fitr

The Sadaqat al-Fitr is also known as Zakat al-Fitr or Fitrana. It is an obligatory payment made by every Muslim who owns the Nisab or its value. It becomes obligatory (Wajib) on the day of `Id al-Fitr at the starting time of the Fajr prayer (i.e. dawn) and it must be paid before performing the `Id prayer. It can also be paid in advance, several days before `Id al-Fitr.

The Sadaqat al-Fitr is a gift to the poor, which Allah has made obligatory at the end of the month of Ramadan. If we pay this, then Allah forgives the mistakes we made in our fasting during the holy month of Ramadan.

The amount to be given is either 1.6 kg of flour or 3.2 kg of dates or barley, but it is permissible to give money instead (i.e. £4). Adults give this money on behalf of their children. If someone misses the payment, they will need to make up for it by paying it later.

The Qurbani

On the day of `Id al-Adha (the festival of sacrifice), it is obligatory (Wajib) to sacrifice an animal. Sacrificing an animal is called Qurbani or Udhiyyah, and it is obligatory on every adult Muslim who owns the Nisab. Sacrificing an animal on this day is to remember how Prophet Ibrahim عليه السلام was ready to sacrifice his son Prophet Isma'il عليه السلام for the sake of Allah.

The sacrifice is performed after the `Id prayer. A goat, sheep, cow or camel can be sacrificed. If it is not possible to sacrifice an animal, it is permissible to send money for it to be performed somewhere else on your behalf.

Sacrificing a goat or a sheep is equal to one share, whereas sacrificing a cow or a camel are equal to seven. The meat can be given to relatives, friends and the poor. Normally, one-third is given to the poor, one-third is given to one's relatives and neighbours and one-third is kept for one's family.

Sadaqah (Charity)

Giving charity (Sadaqah) is an important part of being a Muslim. It is an act that can be done throughout the year without any limits. Some examples of charity (Sadaqah) are:

Buying food packs for the poor.

Looking after an orphan.

Funding a water pump or well for a village.

Sponsoring someone's education (such as memorising the Qur'an).

Supporting educational projects.

Building a house for a homeless person or family.

Paying for someone's medical bills or operation.

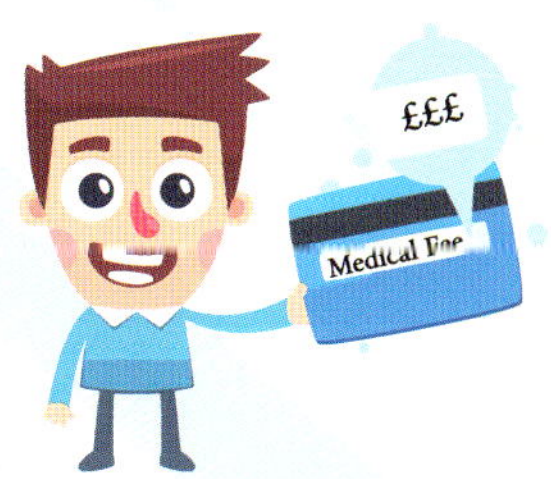

Donating money for good causes such as the ones above is the most common understanding of charity. But in Islam, charity (Sadaqah) has a wider meaning, and it does not just mean giving money for a good cause.

Prophet Muhammad ﷺ explained that every bone in our body should be doing Sadaqah when we get up in the morning (Abu Dawud).

In this hadith, Sadaqah does not mean just giving money, but it is the good deeds a person does throughout the day. Every part of our body should be involved in doing some good deed. This is the reason why the Prophet ﷺ gave a wider meaning to charity by saying that every **good act (ma`ruf)** a person does is a Sadaqah (al-Bukhari).

Some examples of good acts (ma`ruf) that count as Sadaqah in Islam are the following:

- Greeting someone when you meet them.
- Telling others to do good deeds.
- Stopping others from doing bad deeds.
- Removing a harmful object from the road or pathway.

- Reciting the Tasbih (i.e. Subhaanallah).

سُبْحَانَ اللّٰهِ

- Reciting the Takbir (i.e. Allaahu Akbar).

اَللّٰهُ أَكْبَرُ

- Reciting the Tahmid (i.e. Al-hamdu lillaah).

اَلْحَمْدُ لِلّٰهِ

- Reciting the Tahlil (i.e. Laa ilaaha illallaah) .

لَا إِلٰهَ إِلَّا اللّٰهُ

Lesson 21

Rightly Guided Caliphs – `Uthman and `Ali

The Third Rightly Guided Caliph: `Uthman al-Ghani

His name is `Uthman bin al-`Affan. He was among the first Muslims to enter Islam and was among the travellers to go to Abyssinia. He was from the Banu Umayyah and was first married to the Prophet's daughter Ruqayyah, and then, after her death, to the Prophet's third daughter Umm Kulthum. He was known by the honourable title of 'Dhu an-Nurayn' (The Possessor of the Two Lights).

His Virtues and Excellence

Some of the virtues of `Uthman al-Ghani are related below:

- Jabir relates that a funeral was brought before the Prophet ﷺ. However, the Prophet ﷺ did not pray

over the body. Someone asked, "O Messenger of Allah, we have never seen you not pray over someone before." The Prophet ﷺ said, "He used to hate `Uthman." (at-Tirmidhi)

- When Umm Kulthum passed away, the Prophet ﷺ announced, "Marry `Uthman; for if I had a third daughter (to marry off), I would have married her to him. I did not marry my daughters to him except after (receiving permission from Allah through) revelation." (at-Tabarani)

- Abu Hurayra relates that he heard the Prophet ﷺ say, "There will be troubles and mischief." We asked the Prophet ﷺ what we should do at that time, and he said, "Follow your leader and his companions." And he pointed to `Uthman (al-Hakim).

Moments from His Life

`Uthman al-Ghani played an important role in serving the cause of Islam. He was an extremely generous person who spent much of his wealth helping the weak and the poor. Because he had a lot of wealth, he was given the title of 'al-Ghani' (The Rich).

During the caliphate of Abu Bakr, the people of Madinah were suffering from a shortage of food because there was a severe drought. They went to the Caliph Abu Bakr, but he told them to remain patient and to wait for Allah's help. The people did not wait long before one hundred camels loaded with large stock of grain entered Madinah. This large stock of food, which was bought from Syria, belonged to `Uthman.

When all the stock of food was gathered together in `Uthman's house, the merchants came to him and said, "There is a drought and it has been a long time since it has rained. No vegetation grows, and people are suffering severely. Please sell the grain to us so that we may pass it on to the poor people of this city."

Hearing their plight, `Uthman welcomed them into his house and told them to buy whatever they wanted. He then asked them, "How much profit will you give me?"

"For every ten, I will pay you twelve," said one person.

"No, for every ten, I will pay you fourteen," said another.

"No, for every ten, I will pay you fifteen," said a third.

`Uthman replied, "Increase me in profit."

"But there are no other merchants in Madinah besides us," they complained, "who will give you more than that?"

Smiling, `Uthman said, "For one dirham (silver coin), Allah will give me ten. Can any of you beat that?"

"No," replied the merchants.

"Then, I bear witness to Allah that I make this a Sadaqah (donation) to the poor people of Madinah!" said 'Uthman. (Imam al-Ajurri in Kitab ash-Shari`ah)

Another example of `Uthman's generosity was when he bought the well of Roma.

After the Prophet ﷺ and his Companions travelled to Madinah, they did not enjoy the taste of the water in Madinah because they were used to drinking the Zamzam water in Makkah. However, there was one well where the water was sweet, but it was owned by a Jew. The Jew did not want the Muslims to drink from this water for free, so he used to charge them a lot of money to drink water from his well. The Prophet ﷺ asked if anyone would buy the well from the Jew and gift it to the Muslims as charity.

On this occasion, `Uthman came to the rescue. He bought the well from the Jew for 35,000 Dirhams (silver coins). `Uthman gifted this well to the Muslims and allowed everyone, including the non-Muslims, to drink from the well. The Holy Prophet ﷺ was very happy with `Uthman for this great act of generosity and promised him that he will get Paradise as a reward (al-Bukhari).

Regarding `Uthman's death, Ibn `Umar relates that one day `Uthman got up in the morning and told everyone, "I have seen the Prophet ﷺ in my dream last night and he said to me, 'O `Uthman, you will be breaking your fast with us today.'" So `Uthman kept a fast that day knowing it will be his last. Later that day, he was martyred, and he died while fasting (al-Hakim).

The Fourth Rightly Guided Caliph: `Ali al-Murtada

His name is `Ali bin Abi Talib. His father, Abu Talib, was the Prophet's dear uncle and protector. He was a child when he accepted the Prophet's message and was among the very first people to become Muslim. He was brought up in the Prophet's house and later he married the Prophet's younger daughter, Fatimah. He is known as al-Murtada (The Pleased One) and he was the last of the four Rightly Guided Caliphs.

His Virtues and Excellence

Some of the virtues of `Ali bin Abi Talib are given below.

- Sa`d bin Abi Waqqas relates that the Prophet ﷺ said, "O `Ali, are you not pleased that you are to me like the way Prophet Harun عليه السلام was to Prophet Musa عليه السلام? Except that there will be no prophet after me." (al-Bukhari and Muslim)

- Ibn `Umar relates that the Prophet ﷺ said to `Ali, "You are my brother in this life and the next." (at-Tirmidhi).

- `Ali said that the Prophet ﷺ once said to him, "No one loves you except a believer and no one hates you except a hypocrite." (Muslim and at-Tirmidhi)

- Salman al-Farisi relates that the Prophet ﷺ said to `Ali, "The one who loves you (O `Ali) loves me and the one who hates you hates me." (at-Tabarani)

- Ibn `Abbas relates that the Prophet ﷺ said, "I am the city of knowledge and `Ali is its gate. So, whoever wishes to enter the city let him come through its gate." (al-Hakim)

Moments from His Life

There are many inspirational moments from the life of the fourth Rightly Guided Caliph. Some of them are related below.

One day, the Caliph `Ali bin Abi Talib went to the market where he came across a Christian who was selling a shield. He recognised that shield straightaway and said, "This is my shield!" The Christian was adamant that the shield belonged to him, so they decided to go to Qadi Shurayh, the chief judge of the Muslims, to settle the matter.

When they entered the court, Qadi Shurayh stood up for the Caliph and seated him in his place. He then sat at the feet of the Caliph and next to the Christian. `Ali asked Qadi Shurayh to judge between them saying that he lost this shield some time ago and that he did not sell it or give it to anyone.

Qadi Shurayh asked the Christian, "What do you say about the Caliph's claim?"

The man answered: "This is my shield and the Caliph is lying."

The judge then asked `Ali, "O Caliph, do you have any proof that the shield is yours?" `Ali smiled and said that he did not. So, Qadi Shurayh gave his verdict in favour of the Christian.

Seeing this display of justice and fairness, the Christian said, "I declare that such are the rulings of Prophets! The Caliph took me to his court, where his judge gave a verdict against him! I hereby declare that there is no God but Allah, and that Muhammad is His servant and Messenger. The shield is yours, Caliph. I followed the army and the shield dropped from your camel."

`Ali then answered, "Now that you have embraced Islam, the shield is yours; you can keep it." (al-Bayhaqi in as-Sunan al-Kubra)

Once, during the Siege of Khaybar, `Ali bin Abi Talib remained behind because he was suffering from eye trouble. He said to himself, "How can I remain behind, and not be with the Prophet ﷺ." So, he decided to set out and join the Prophet ﷺ.

On the day before the conquest of Khaybar, the Prophet ﷺ said, "Tomorrow I will give this flag to a man through whose hands Allah will give us victory. He loves Allah and His Prophet, and he is loved by Allah and His Prophet."

The people remained awake that night wondering who would take this flag. On the next day, everyone went to the Prophet ﷺ eagerly waiting and hoping that they would receive the flag. The Prophet ﷺ said, "Where is `Ali bin Abi Talib?"

The Companions told him that `Ali was suffering from an eye problem. The Prophet ﷺ called for him. When `Ali came, the Prophet ﷺ spat in his eye and prayed to Allah to cure his eyes. Miraculously, `Ali was cured and it was as if he never had any problems

with his eye in the first place. Then the Prophet ﷺ gave him the flag (al-Bukhari).

On the day of the Conquest of Khaybar, `Ali was holding the flag given to him by the Prophet ﷺ. He made his way to the enemy's fortress and fought with their soldiers. As he was fighting bravely, he dropped his shield on the floor. So, he took a broken door from the fortress and used it as a shield. He kept on fighting the enemy and shielding himself with this door until he conquered the fortress. Then he threw that door on the floor. Abu Rafi` relates that he and seven other men tried to move that door from its place, but they were unable to move it (Ahmad).

Lesson 22

The Minor Signs of the Day of Judgement

Allah has blessed Prophet Muhammad ﷺ with perfect knowledge. The Prophet ﷺ was given the knowledge of the first and the last. `Umar bin al-Khattab narrates that one day, the Prophet ﷺ stood up and told the Companions everything that took place since the beginning of creation to everything that will take place until the people of Heaven enter Heaven and the people of Hell enter Hell (al-Bukhari).

Describing the amount of the Prophet's knowledge, Hudhayfah said that the Prophet ﷺ got up on his pulpit and gave a speech to the Companions telling them everything that will take place until the Day of Judgment. He said that the Prophet ﷺ did not leave out anything and he told them about everything that will take place (al-Bukhari and Muslim).

In another narration, `Amr bin Akhtab said that the most knowledgeable person among them was the person who was the best to memorise everything the Prophet ﷺ said.

The Prophet ﷺ was given knowledge of the future. He foretold many of the great events that would take place within his Ummah. Some of the major events in the future that the Prophet ﷺ foretold are:

- **The Conquest of Jerusalem (637 CE/16 AH):** The Prophet ﷺ passed away in the year 632 CE and Jerusalem was conquered by the Companions during the caliphate of `Umar bin al-Khattab in April 637 CE. This was foretold by the Prophet ﷺ when he counted this as one of the six signs of the Day of Judgement (al-Bukhari).

- **The End of the Rightly Guided Caliphate and the Rise of Kingship in Islam (661 CE/41 AH):** The Prophet ﷺ said, "The Caliphate will be in my Ummah for thirty years, then there will be kingship after that." (at-Tirmidhi) The caliphates of Abu Bakr as-Siddiq, `Umar al-Faruq, `Uthman al-Ghani and `Ali al-Murtada came to roughly thirty years.

- **The Great Fire in the Hijaz (1256 CE/654 AH):** The Prophet ﷺ said, "The Day of Judgement will not be established till a fire will come out of the land of Hijaz, and it will throw light on the necks of the camels at Bosra (Syria)." (al-Bukhari and Muslim)

  A great volcanic eruption took place near Madinah in a place called Harrat Rahat in the year 1256 CE/654 AH. The lava flowed 23 km towards Madinah. The people of Madinah got worried because it was a great volcanic eruption never seen before. According to the historians, the men, women and children took refuge in the Prophet's mosque and encircled the Prophet's grave seeking Allah's help and deliverance. When the lava reached the borders of Madinah, it stopped and went the other direction away from the Prophet's mosque.

- **The Mongol Invasion (1258 CE/656 AH):** The Prophet ﷺ said, "The Day of Judgement will not be established until you fight with the Turks; people with small eyes, red faces and flat noses. Their faces will look like shields coated with leather. The Day of Judgement will not be established till you fight with people whose shoes are made of hair." (al-Bukhari)

- **The Conquest of Constantinople (1453 CE/857 AH):** The Prophet ﷺ said, "You will certainly conquer Constantinople, and what an excellent leader is its leader, and what an excellent army is that army." (Ahmad) The great commander and 7th Ottoman ruler, Muhammad al-Fatih, conquered Constantinople at the age of 21. He was a great Muslim leader who supported the cause of Islam and expanded Muslim rule over East Europe.

Among the most important things that the Prophet ﷺ told us about were the signs of the Day of the Judgement.

We must believe in the signs of the Last Day. It is an important part of our belief in the Day of Judgement. There are many signs of the Day of Judgement and they are divided into two categories: the **minor signs** and the **major signs**.

The minor signs take place over a long period of time. Some of the minor signs have passed and others are yet to come, and many of the minor signs are even taking place today.

When we see these signs, we should not be scared or worried. Rather, we should become stronger in our faith and understand that these are from the signs of the Day of Judgement. Some of the minor signs that are taking place in our age are detailed below.

- Children will become angry quickly and not listen to their parents.
- People will compete with one another in building tall buildings.

  For example, today we see tall buildings in the Arabian Peninsula. Over 50 years ago, the people who lived in these areas were very poor shepherds who roamed the deserts without shoes. But today they have a lot of money and now are competing among themselves to build the tallest buildings in the world, like the Burj Khalifa in Dubai.

- There will be much killing.
- Ignorance will become widespread and knowledge will be taken away.
- Practicing religion will be very hard like holding onto a hot piece of coal.
- A person will be a believer in the morning and by evening he will be a disbeliever.

- People will compete with one another in building mosques.

- The buildings of Makkah will rise higher than its mountains and tunnels will be built through the city.

  For example, the Abraj Al-Bait Towers (the Clock Tower) in Makkah is the third tallest building in the world. Over 50 years ago, there was not even one building taller than the minarets of the two holy mosques in Makkah and Madinah.

- Mountains will be removed from their place.

  For example, in Makkah, some of the mountains were destroyed to put tall buildings in their place.

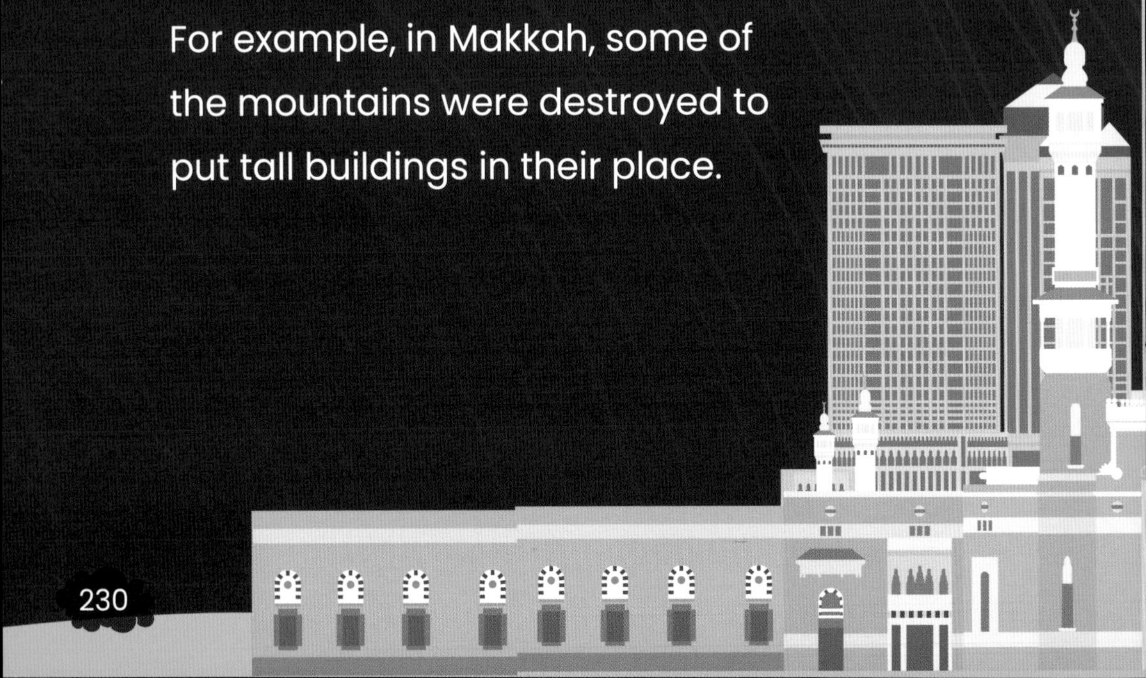

- There will be acid in the rain.
- Wicked people will spread widely.

  For example, people who become famous through the media for doing bad things.
- People will trust those who lie but not trust those who are honest.
- The truthful will be called a liar and the liar will be called truthful.
- Mosques will be beautiful, but the hearts will be ugly.

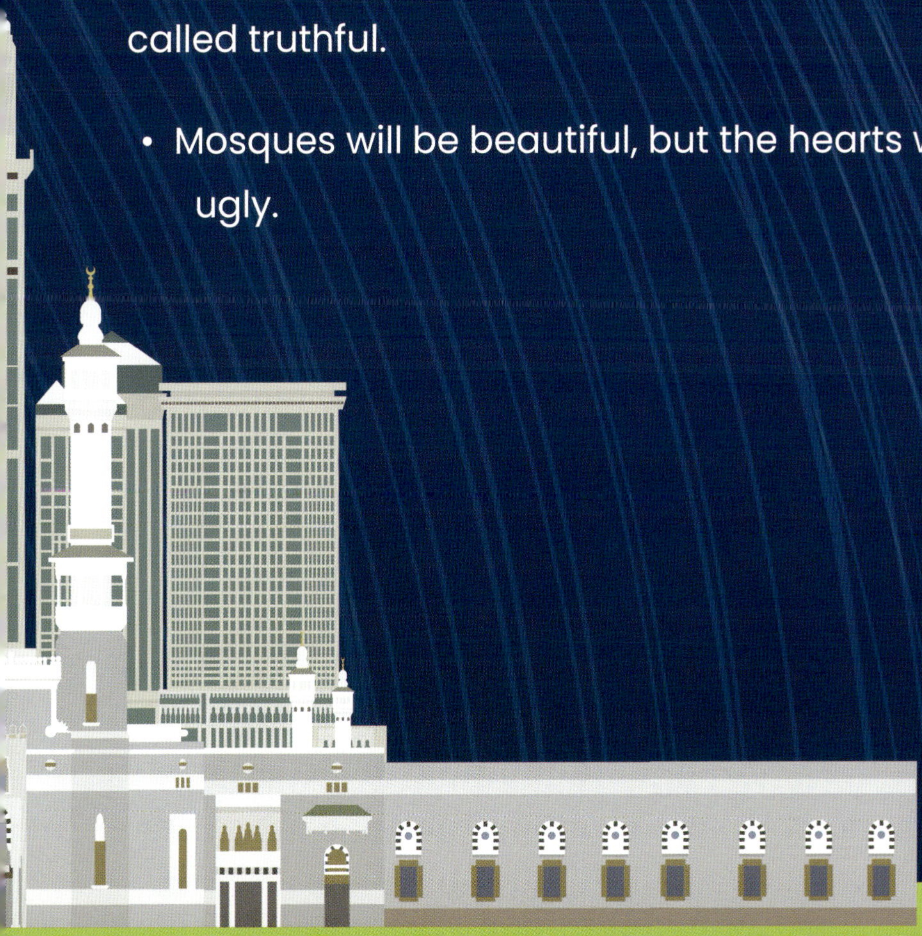

- Men will marry men and women will marry women.
- Many children will be born outside marriage.
- Musical instruments will be widespread.

  For example, modern technological devices that play music can be found everywhere.
- There will be a lot of alcoholic drinks.
- People will mock and make fun of others a lot.

  For example, mean and nasty comments people make about others online.

We can see all these signs of the Day of Judgement taking place today. This shows us the truthfulness of Prophet Muhammad ﷺ, who foretold us these signs more than 1400 years ago.

We are living in the age of the Minor Signs of the Day of Judgement. This means that the age we are living in is a time of evil and corruption. So, we need to be more careful in protecting our faith. Every time we see these signs, we should ask Allah for His forgiveness and pray for steadfastness in our religion.

Lesson 23

Ahl al-Bayt – Fatimah and al-Hasanayn

Sayyidah Fatimah az-Zahra'

Sayyidah Fatimah az-Zahra' is the youngest daughter of the Prophet ﷺ. She is the mother of Imam al-Hasan and Imam al-Husayn. She was given the title of **az-Zahra'** (The Lady of Light) and **al-Batul** (the Pure). She is the leader of all the women of Paradise and she is among the greatest women of Islam.

Her Virtues and Excellence

Some of the virtues of Sayyidah Fatimah az-Zahra' are related below.

- Al-Miswar bin Makhrama relates that the Prophet ﷺ said, "Fatimah is a part of me. Whoever angers her, angers me." (al-Bukhari and Muslim)

- Thawban narrates that the last person the Prophet ﷺ would meet from his family before setting off on his journey was Fatimah. The first person he would meet upon his return would also be Fatimah (Abu Dawud and Ahmad).

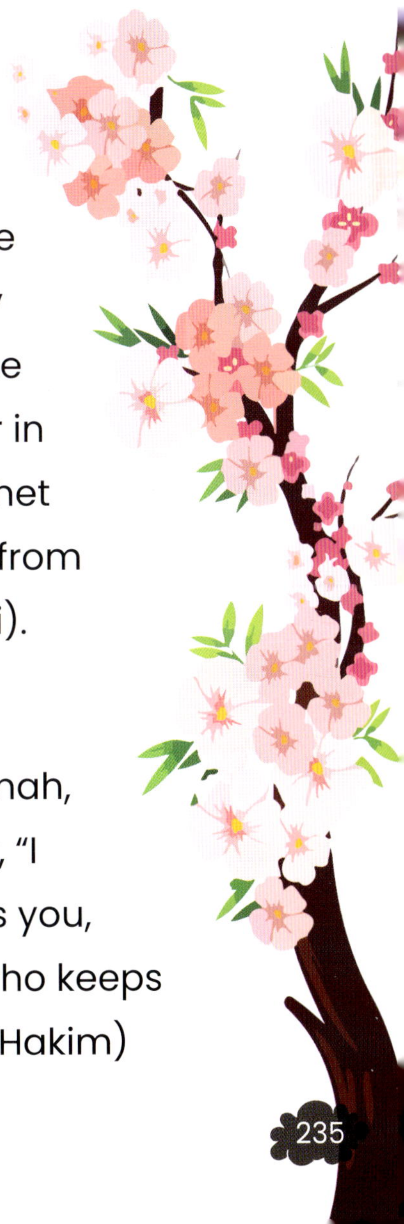

- Mother of the Believers `A'ishah relates that whenever Sayyidah Fatimah would enter the room, the Prophet ﷺ would welcome her by getting up and kissing her. Then he would take her hand and seat her in his place. And whenever the Prophet ﷺ would enter, she would get up from her place and kiss him (an-Nasa'i).

- Abu Hurayrah narrates that the Prophet ﷺ would look at `Ali, Fatimah, al-Hasan and al-Husayn and say, "I am at war with the one who fights you, and I am at peace with the one who keeps peace with you." (Ahmad and al-Hakim)

- Mother of the Believers `A'ishah said, "I never saw anyone more like the Messenger of Allah ﷺ in respect of silence and speech, and his sitting and standing, than Fatimah." (at-Tirmidhi and Abu Dawud)

Moments from Her Life

Some moments from her life have been detailed below.

Once when Imam al-Hasan and Imam al-Husayn were young, they became very sick. They were so ill that the Prophet ﷺ came to visit them. The Prophet ﷺ suggested to `Ali, their father, that they should all fast for three days and pray to Allah to make them better. So, `Ali, Fatimah and their servant decided to act upon the Prophet's advice and fast for three days.

Imam `Ali and Sayyidah Fatimah did not have much wealth and they did not have any food in the house. So, Imam `Ali borrowed some food from a Jewish man and Sayyidah Fatimah prepared five loaves of flat bread to break their fast. As they sat down and placed the bread in front of them to break their fast, there was a knock on the door. A man greeted them saying, "Peace be upon you, O family of the Prophet. I am a poor man, so please feed me for the sake of Allah and Allah will feed you in Paradise."

So, they gave their bread to him, and because there was not any other food in the house, they had to break their fast with water. They went to sleep hungry that night.

On the next day, they fasted again. When the time of breaking the fast arrived, they had prepared some food and laid it down in front of them. Before they could eat, there was a knock on the door. An

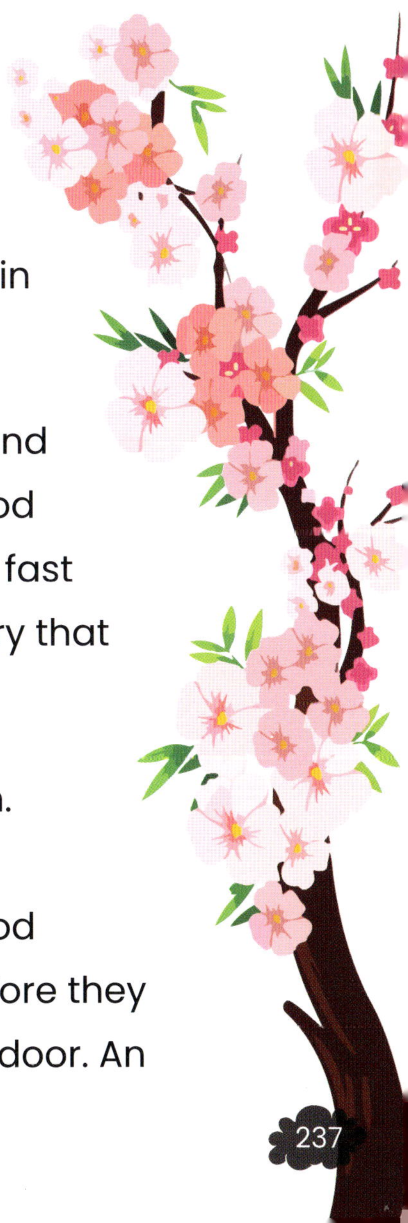

orphan boy was standing there, and he was asking for food. They gave their bread to him and broke their fast again with water. They went to sleep another night hungry without eating anything.

On the third day, they fasted again. When the time of breaking the fast arrived, there was a knock on the door again. This time it was a freed prisoner and he was asking them for food. Imam `Ali and Sayyidah Fatimah gave the bread they prepared to the freed prisoner and they broke their fast with water for a third day in a row.

In the morning, the next day, Imam `Ali took his two sons al-Hasan and al-Husayn and went to see the Prophet ﷺ. When the Prophet ﷺ saw them trembling with extreme hunger, he said, "Nothing hurts me more than to see you like this." Then the Prophet ﷺ went to their home and saw Sayyidah Fatimah sitting there, her stomach looked as though it was joined to her back and her eyes were sunk into their sockets. This was painful for the Prophet ﷺ to see.

At that moment, Angel Jibra'il came down to the Prophet ﷺ, and recited the verse, "*And they give (their own) food, in deep love of Allah, to the needy, the orphan and prisoner (out of sacrifice, despite their own need for it), (And say:) 'We are feeding you only to please Allah. We do not seek any reward from you nor (wish for) any thanks.'*" (al-Insan 76:7-9) He congratulated the Ahl al-Bayt for their patience and sacrifice. And some of the scholars said that this verse was revealed in their honour due to their selflessness and sacrifice.

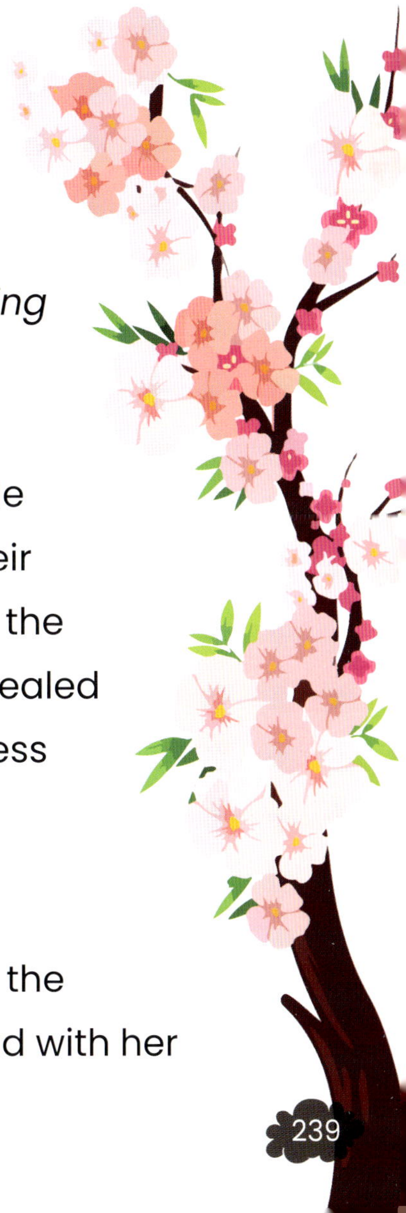

Mother of the Believers `A'ishah narrates another incident regarding the final moments Sayyidah Fatimah had with her beloved father, the Prophet of Allah. She narrates that when Sayyidah Fatimah visited the Prophet ﷺ, he greeted her and sat her beside him. Then, he told her something in secret and she cried. Then the Prophet ﷺ told her something else in secret and she smiled. Mother of the Believers `A'ishah asked her about this, but she did not want to reveal the Prophet's secret.

When the Prophet ﷺ passed away, Mother of the Believers `A'ishah asked Sayyidah Fatimah about the incident again, and she said, "The Prophet ﷺ told me in secret that Angel Jibra'il would review the Qur'an with him once every year, but this year he reviewed it with him twice. He said that this means his time to leave this world had come. Then he told me that I would be the first person to join him from among his family. Hearing this, I cried. Then he said to me, 'Are you not pleased that you are the leader of the women in Paradise.' So, I smiled when I heard that." (al-Bukhari and Muslim)

Imam al-Hasan and Imam al-Husayn

Imam al-Hasan and Imam al-Husayn are the beloved grandsons of the Prophet ﷺ. They are the sons of `Ali bin Abi Talib and Fatimah az-Zahra'. The term '**al-Hasanayn**' is sometimes used to refer to both of the Imams.

After the period of the Rightly Guided Caliphs, both Imams played an important role in keeping safe the integrity and unity of the Muslims. They gave their lives for the sake of Allah, and Muslims all around the world remember their sacrifices to this day.

Their Virtues and Excellence

Some of the virtues and excellence of Imam al-Hasan and Imam al-Husayn are related below.

- Ibn `Umar reports that the Prophet ﷺ said, "Al-Hasan and al-Husayn are my two flowers from the world." (at-Tirmidhi, an-Nasa'i and Ahmad)

- Abu Hurayrah relates that the Prophet ﷺ said, "Whoever loves al-Hasan and al-Husayn has loved me, and whoever hates them has hated me." (Ibn Majah, an-Nasa'i and Ahmad)

- `Ali al-Murtada reports that the Prophet ﷺ informed him that he, Fatimah and al-Hasan and al-Husayn will be the first people to enter Paradise. Imam `Ali asked, "And what about those who love us?" The Prophet ﷺ replied, "They will be behind you." (al-Hakim)

- Hudhayfah relates that the Prophet ﷺ said, "Indeed, an angel that has never come down to the earth before this night asked Allah for permission to meet me and give me the glad tidings that Fatimah is the leader of the women of

Paradise and that al-Hasan and al-Husayn are the two leaders of the youth of Paradise." (at-Tirmidhi, an-Nasa'i and Ahmad)

Moments from Their Life

Some glimpses of their life and their close bond with their grandfather, the Prophet of Allah, have been detailed below.

One day Sayyidah Fatimah brought the two Imams to the Prophet ﷺ and asked if they will inherit anything from him. The Prophet ﷺ said, "As for al-Hasan, he will inherit my awe and leadership; and as for al-Husayn, he will inherit my courage and generosity." (at-Tabarani)

Ibn Shaddad narrates from his father that the Prophet ﷺ came out one day to offer the `Isha' prayer while he was carrying either al-Hasan or al-Husayn. The Prophet ﷺ

placed him on the floor next to him and then started the prayer. As he was offering the prayer, the Prophet ﷺ lengthened the prostration for a long time.

Ibn Shaddad's father said that he raised his head to see what was happening. He saw the young child playing on the Prophet's back, so he quickly returned to the prostration. After the prayer, the people asked why the Prophet ﷺ lengthened his prostration and he told them that his young grandson was on his back playing, and he did not want to stop him from playing (an-Nasa'i).

Talking about the Prophet's love and affection for them, Abu Hurayrah narrates that one day the Prophet ﷺ was delivering the sermon, when al-Hasan and al-Husayn entered the mosque both wearing red shirts. When he saw them, the Prophet ﷺ came down from the pulpit and carried them and placed them both on his lap. He kept them with him on his lap while he continued delivering the sermon (at-Tirmidhi and an-Nasa'i).

Sa`d bin Abi Waqqas states that when the verse, *"Come, let us (jointly) call our sons and your sons, our women and your women, and ourselves and yourselves (at the same place)"* (Al `Imran 3:61), was revealed, the Prophet ﷺ called `Ali, Fatimah, al-Hasan and al-Husayn, and said, "O Allah, these are my family." (Muslim and at-Tirmidhi)

It was the practice of the Prophet ﷺ that he would give al-Hasan and al-Husayn a ride on his back. He would play with them and spend time with them. One day, as the Prophet ﷺ was giving al-Hasan and al-Husayn a ride on his back, `Umar bin al-Khattab said to them, "What an excellent ride you two have!" And the Prophet ﷺ replied, "Yes, and what excellent riders they are!" (al-Bazzar)

Lesson 24

The Major Signs of the Day of Judgement

As the Day of Judgement comes closer, the signs which show us that it is approaching will become even greater. We are currently living in the time of the **minor signs**, but eventually after a long time this stage will pass, and a new stage will begin. This new stage will be the time of the **major signs** of the Day of Judgement, and its beginning will be marked by the appearance of the 'Awaited Imam', Imam Muhammad al-Mahdi.

During the time of the major signs, the tests and troubles in the world will be greater than before. Every time a sign appears it will show that the end of times is fast approaching. Those people whose faith in the unseen is weak, think that some of the major signs are questionable and unbelievable. However, when they happen, it will show a clear proof of the truthfulness of Islam and the certainty of the Day of Judgement.

Some of the major signs are detailed below. It must be kept in mind that these signs will appear together and will follow one after the other in a short period of time.

The Appearance of al-Imam al-Mahdi

The appearance of al-Imam al-Mahdi will be the first major sign of the Day of Judgement. Al-Imam al-Mahdi means '**the Guided Imam**', and this is because he will be a great Muslim leader who will bring peace and harmony to the world. He will unite the Muslims during a time of much fighting and troubles amongst the people, and he will bring justice and order to their lands.

His name will be **Muhammad** and his father's name will be **`Abd Allah**. He will be a direct descendent of Prophet Muhammad ﷺ and he will be born in Madinah. He will have a beautiful face and on his right cheek there will be a beauty spot.

He will be recognised in Makkah and the Muslims will pledge allegiance to him in the Holy Mosque. Hearing this, an army will come from Syria to capture him, but when it is on its way it will be swallowed by the earth. Everyone will then recognise this as a sign that he is truly the Imam that they had been waiting for.

Before the appearance of Imam Muhammad al-Mahdi there will be some signs that will take place. Among them are the appearance of a comet from the east, two lunar eclipses during the month of Ramadan and violent bloodshed at the plains of `Arafat during the days of Hajj.

The Emergence of ad-Dajjal

The Prophet ﷺ foretold the appearance of a man from the east who will be a great liar and deceiver. He named this person as **al-Masih ad-Dajjal (the False Messiah/the Antichrist)** and described him as being one-eyed, because his right eye will be defective. The Prophet ﷺ said that the word '**kafir**' (disbeliever) will be written on his head. Every believing person will be able to see this on his forehead, even if they cannot read or write.

Ad-Dajjal will travel around the world calling people to follow him. First, he will claim that he is a prophet, then he will claim that he is God. He will have many supernatural powers. Wealth will follow him, and he will give it to his followers. Whoever rejects him will be stricken with difficulty and famine.

The test of ad-Dajjal will be one of the most difficult, because he will present Paradise as the Hellfire and the Hellfire as Paradise. He will show both Paradise and Hell to the people, those who enter his paradise will really enter the Hellfire, while those who enter his hellfire will really enter Paradise.

He will go to every town and city, and those people who have weak Iman (faith) will follow him. However, ad-Dajjal will not be able to enter Makkah or Madinah because they will be guarded by angels. So instead, he will send an earthquake which will force the hypocrites to leave Makkah and Madinah and to follow him.

As Muslims, we must pray to Allah for protection from the test of al-Masih ad-Dajjal (the False Messiah/the Antichrist).

The Return of Prophet `Isa عليه السلام

During the days of ad-Dajjal, Prophet `Isa عليه السلام will return to earth. He will come down from the heavens at the white minaret in the eastern side of Damascus, placing his hands on the wings of two angels. He will wear two pieces of clothing that are lightly dyed with saffron. When he lowers his head, drops of water will fall from his head, and when he will raise it up, beads like pearls will scatter from it.

Prophet `Isa عليه السلام will meet with the Muslim army at the time of the Fajr prayer. On this day, they will be preparing to go into battle with ad-Dajjal and his army. Once the war starts, Prophet `Isa عليه السلام will search for ad-Dajjal, and when ad-Dajjal sees him, he will try to escape but Prophet `Isa عليه السلام will catch hold of him at the gate of Ludd and will kill him.

After the epic battle is over, Prophet `Isa عليه السلام will rule as a fair leader. There will be so much wealth and it will be shared fairly among the people so that no one will want any more.

Ya`juj wa Ma`juj (Gog and Magog)

After many years of peace, Allah will let out a group of people known as Ya`juj wa Ma`juj (Gog and Magog). They will cause destruction wherever they go. Allah will reveal to Prophet `Isa عليه السلام that it will not be possible to fight them, so he should take his followers to Mount Tur and seek protection there until Allah's command comes.

Prophet `Isa عليه السلام and his followers will pray to Allah for Ya`juj wa Ma`juj's destruction, and so Allah will send an insect that will bite them on their necks. This will cause all of them to be destroyed by the next morning, not even one of them will be left. When Prophet `Isa عليه السلام and his followers come down from the mountain they will find that because of Ya`juj wa Ma`juj the earth will be full of their disgusting smell. So, Allah will send rain which will purify the earth and wash it in a way that it will look as clean as a mirror.

After the earth will be purified, it will have so much blessing that a single pomegranate would grow so big that it would be able to feed a group of people, and a single cow will give enough milk to feed a whole tribe. During this peaceful period, Prophet `Isa عليه السلام will die a natural death and he will be buried next to Prophet Muhammad ﷺ in the blessed and holy of city of Madinah.

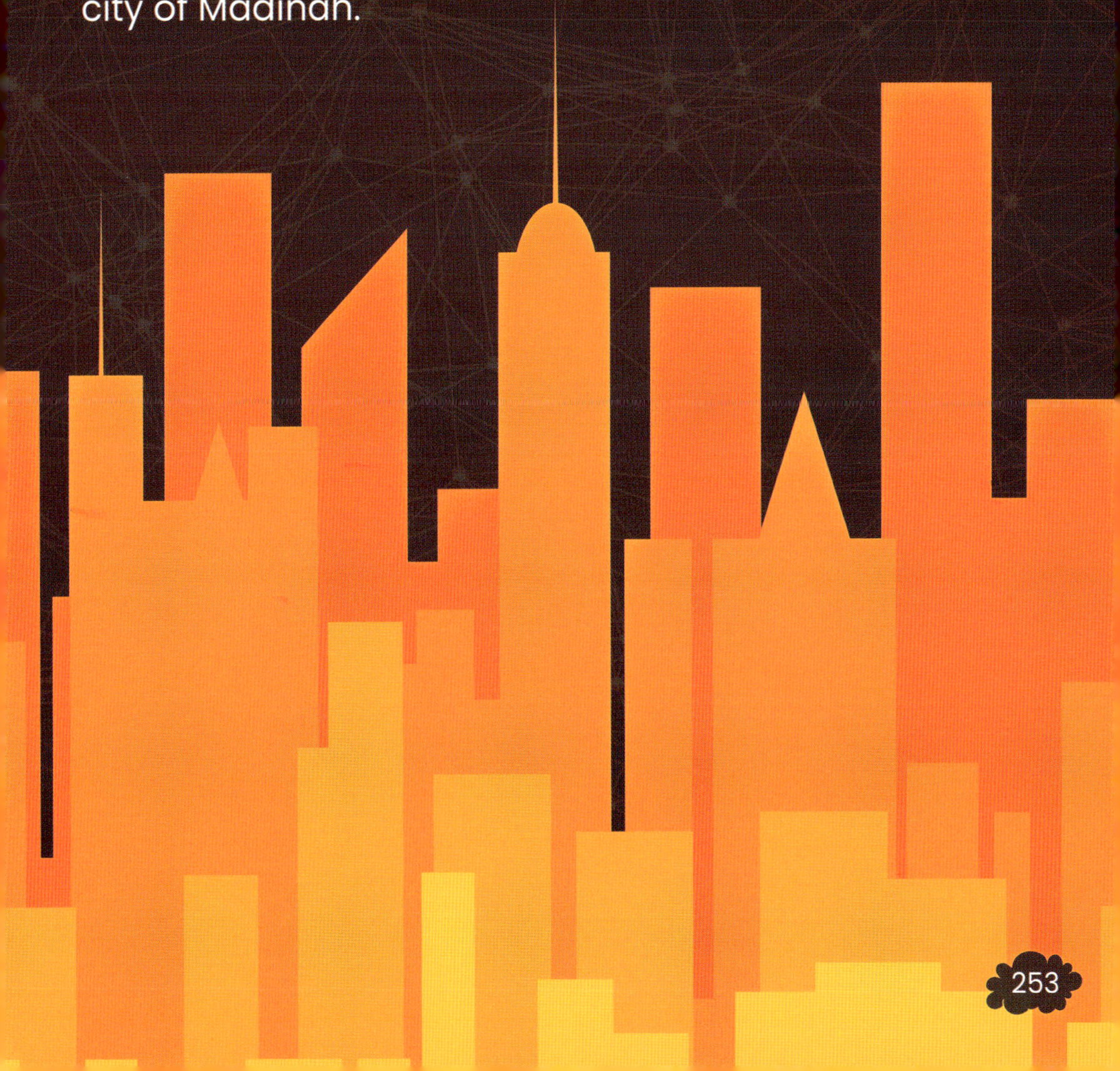

Lesson 25

Hajj and Ziyarah

For a Muslim, performing the Hajj (Pilgrimage) is a journey of a lifetime, which must be done at least once by those people who are able to. It is one of the pillars of Islam.

A pilgrimage is a special journey a person goes on to visit a holy place. Muslims perform the pilgrimage to Makkah to visit the Ka`bah (the House of Allah) and other holy places around Makkah.

In Islam, there are two types of pilgrimages: the major pilgrimage, which is known as **Hajj**, and the minor pilgrimage, which is known as **`Umrah**. The major pilgrimage, Hajj, takes place over five to six days between the 8th and 13th of Dhu al-Hijjah. It can be performed only during these days, and not on any other day of the year. The minor pilgrimage, `Umrah, can be performed throughout the year as many times as a person wants to.

During the Hajj and `Umrah, we perform some important actions known as the **pilgrimage rites (Manasik)**. These rites are in remembrance of Prophet Ibrahim عليه السلام, his wife Sayyidah Hajar and their son Prophet Isma'il عليه السلام. The rites teach us many important lessons such as the value of equality and brotherhood, the value of sacrifice and the value of devotion and dedication to Allah.

All three of these values are shown when we put on the **Ihram** (the two white unsewn sheets). For example, it shows **human equality and brotherhood** because everyone who performs the pilgrimage is wearing the same simple style of clothing. It does not matter if someone is rich or poor, strong or weak; everyone wears these two white sheets. Wearing them shows that we all belong to the same human family and that we are all equal before Allah.

Putting on the Ihram also shows the value of **sacrifice**, because the pilgrims show that they are ready to sacrifice their desires by not cutting their hair, trimming their nails or wearing perfume.

It is a symbolic act which also shows the value of **devotion and dedication to Allah**, because when the pilgrims wear the two white sheets, they make a promise to devote and dedicate their life to Allah.

By keeping to these values, the pilgrimage becomes a turning point in a Muslim's life and helps them to become a better person.

The Days of Hajj

Muslims come from all over the world to perform the Hajj. They arrive in Makkah either during the month of Dhu al-Qa`dah or the first week of Dhu al-Hijjah.

Before reaching the **Miqat** (the boundary around Makkah which the pilgrim cannot pass except in the state of Ihram), they put on the Ihram. When putting on the Ihram, the pilgrim makes an **intention** to perform the Hajj, saying:

اَللّٰهُمَّ إِنِّيْ أُرِيْدُ الْحَجَّ فَيَسِّرْهُ لِيْ وَتَقَبَّلْهُ مِنِّيْ

O Allah, I intend to perform the Pilgrimage, so make it easy for me and accept it from me.

Then the **Talbiyyah** is uttered:

لَبَّيْكَ اَللّٰهُمَّ لَبَّيْكَ. لَبَّيْكَ لَا شَرِيْكَ لَكَ لَبَّيْكَ. إِنَّ الْحَمْدَ وَالنِّعْمَةَ لَكَ وَالْمُلْكَ لَا شَرِيْكَ لَكَ

Here I am at Your service, O Lord, here I am. Here I am at Your service and You have no partner; here I am. For You alone is all praise and all bounty, and for You alone is the power. You have no partner.

The pilgrims continue reciting the Talbiyyah as they travel to Makkah. When they reach Makkah, the pilgrims make their way to the Ka`bah and perform the `Umrah. During the `Umrah, they walk around the Ka`bah seven times in an act of worship called the '**Tawaf**'. Then they continue to Mount Safa where they perform another act of worship called the '**Sa`i**' which involves running between the Safa and Marwah seven times, ending at Marwah.

When the `Umrah is complete, the pilgrims shave or trim their hair and come out of the state of Ihram. Then they stay in Makkah and wait until the 8th

of Dhu al-Hijjah, when they put their Ihram back on again.

On the 8th of Dhu al-Hijjah (the first day of Hajj), the pilgrims wake up before dawn and put their Ihram on. They perform the Fajr prayer in Makkah, and then set off for **Mina**. They spend their first day and night in Mina and perform five prayers there (i.e. Zuhr, `Asr, Maghrib, `Isha' and Fajr).

On the 9th of Dhu al-Hijjah (the second day of Hajj), after sunrise, the pilgrims make their way to **`Arafat** where they stay from **noon to sunset**. This day is the most important of the five days. If it is missed, then the Hajj is invalid, because being at `Arafat in the state of Ihram on this day is the pillar of the Hajj.

In `Arafat, the pilgrims worship Allah, supplicate to Him and ask Him for forgiveness. Worshipping Allah here is known as '**Wuquf `Arafah**'. They combine the Zuhr and the `Asr prayers and perform them together at the time of Zuhr. They offer this prayer behind the Imam of Hajj, who leads it from inside Masjid an-Namira.

After **sunset**, the pilgrims leave for **Muzdalifa**. When they reach Muzdalifa, they combine the Maghrib and `Isha' prayers and perform them together at the time of `Isha'. They spend the night in Muzdalifa, spending a part of the night remembering and worshipping Allah. During this night, the pilgrims collect **70 small stones** the size of kidney beans to be used for the Rami, the following day.

On the next day, the 10th of Dhu al-Hijjah (the third day of Hajj), the pilgrims perform the Fajr prayer and then leave for Mina before sunrise. From Mina, the pilgrims make their way to the **Jamarat al-`Aqabah** (the third stone pillar) and perform the Rami. The **Rami** is an act of worship where the pilgrim throws seven stones at the pillar while saying the takbir (Allahu Akbar). On this day, stones are only thrown at the third pillar.

After performing the Rami, the pilgrims perform the **animal sacrifice (Qurbani)**. This day is also `Id al-Adha; those Muslims who are not performing the Hajj will be sacrificing an animal as well. Once the Qurbani has been performed, the pilgrim can shave or trim their hair. After this, the Ihram can be removed, and the pilgrim can put on their normal clothes.

Once all these steps are complete, the pilgrims need to return to the Ka`bah within three days and perform the **Tawaf az-Ziyarah** (or **Tawaf al-Ifadah**). This Tawaf is performed normally with no Idtiba` (baring the right shoulder) or Ramal (walking like a wrestler). After completing the Tawaf, two units of prayer are performed behind the Maqam Ibrahim or anywhere in the mosque if space cannot be found near it. Then the pilgrim makes his or her way to Safa to perform the Sa`i. The pilgrim must return to Mina to stay there in the night.

On the 11th of Dhu al-Hijjah (the fourth day of Hajj), the pilgrims remain in Mina. After midday, the Rami is performed. Seven stones are thrown at each of the three pillars (21 stones altogether). The pilgrims spend the night at Mina and wait there till the next day.

On the 12th of Dhu al-Hijjah (the fifth day of Hajj), the pilgrims perform the Rami again after midday. They throw seven stones at each of the three pillars. On this day, the pilgrims have a choice to either remain in Mina for another night or to return to Makkah. If they wish to return to Makkah, then they must leave before sunset.

On the 13th of Dhu al-Hijjah (the last day of Hajj), if the pilgrim has not returned to Makkah and stayed in Mina for the night, then they must perform the Rami again after midday. After the Rami, the Hajj is completed, and they can return to Makkah.

The pilgrims remain in Makkah until the time comes for them to leave. Before leaving, the pilgrim must perform a final Tawaf, which is known as the **Tawaf al-Wada`**. This is a normal Tawaf with no Idtiba` or Ramal. During these final moments, the pilgrims supplicate to Allah and ask to come back again for another visit.

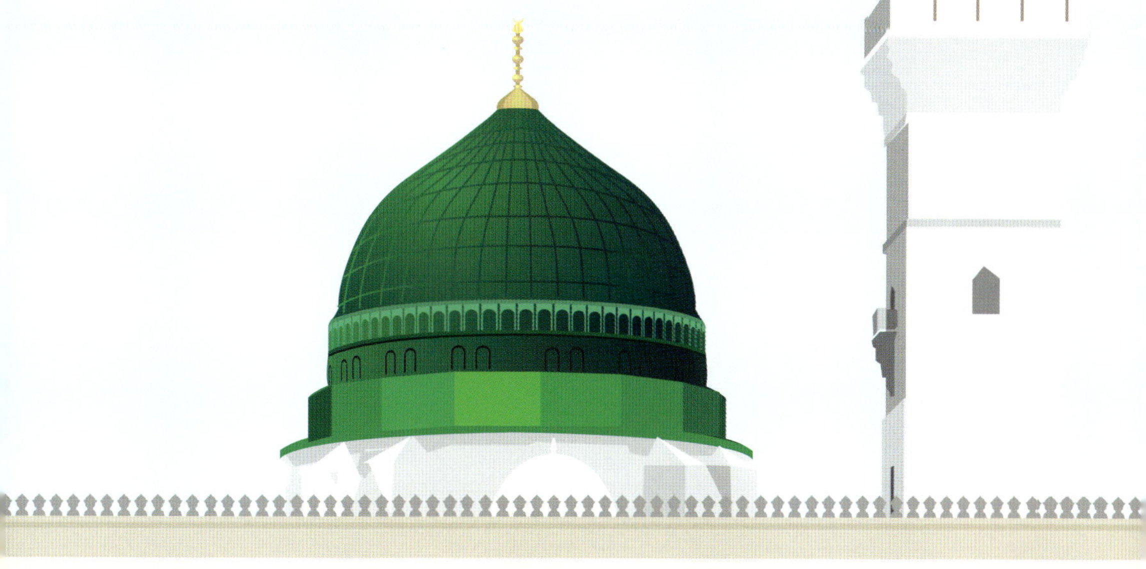

Ziyarah

Before returning home, the pilgrims make an important journey to Madinah. Visiting Madinah is called '**Ziyarah**'. The Ziyarah is not part of the Hajj, but it is an important act of worship which the pilgrims perform.

When the pilgrim goes to Madinah, he or she enters the Prophet's mosque (Masjid an-Nabawi) and performs two units of prayer there. The pilgrim then makes his way to the **Rawdah**, where Prophet Muhammad ﷺ is buried. The pilgrim stands at the golden gates, known as the **Muwajahah**, and greets the Prophet ﷺ.

Inside the Rawdah, the first two Rightly Guided Caliphs, Abu Bakr as-Siddiq and `Umar al-Faruq, are also buried there next to the Prophet ﷺ. After greeting the Prophet ﷺ, the pilgrim greets them as well. Then the pilgrim makes his way to **Jannat al-Baqi**, where many of the Companions and the Ahl al-Bayt are buried and he greets all those who are buried there.

During the stay in Madinah, the pilgrim spends his or her days praying in the Prophet's Mosque (Masjid an-Nabawi) and reciting a lot of salutations on the Prophet ﷺ (Salat `ala an-Nabi ﷺ).

Staying in Madinah is important because it is a time to be close to Prophet Muhammad ﷺ, as the Prophet ﷺ listens to our greetings and replies to them. The more salutations (**Salawat**) and greetings (**Salam**) we send on the Prophet ﷺ, the closer we get to him and the higher our rank is raised by Allah.

العُمْرَة

ROUTE O

البداية

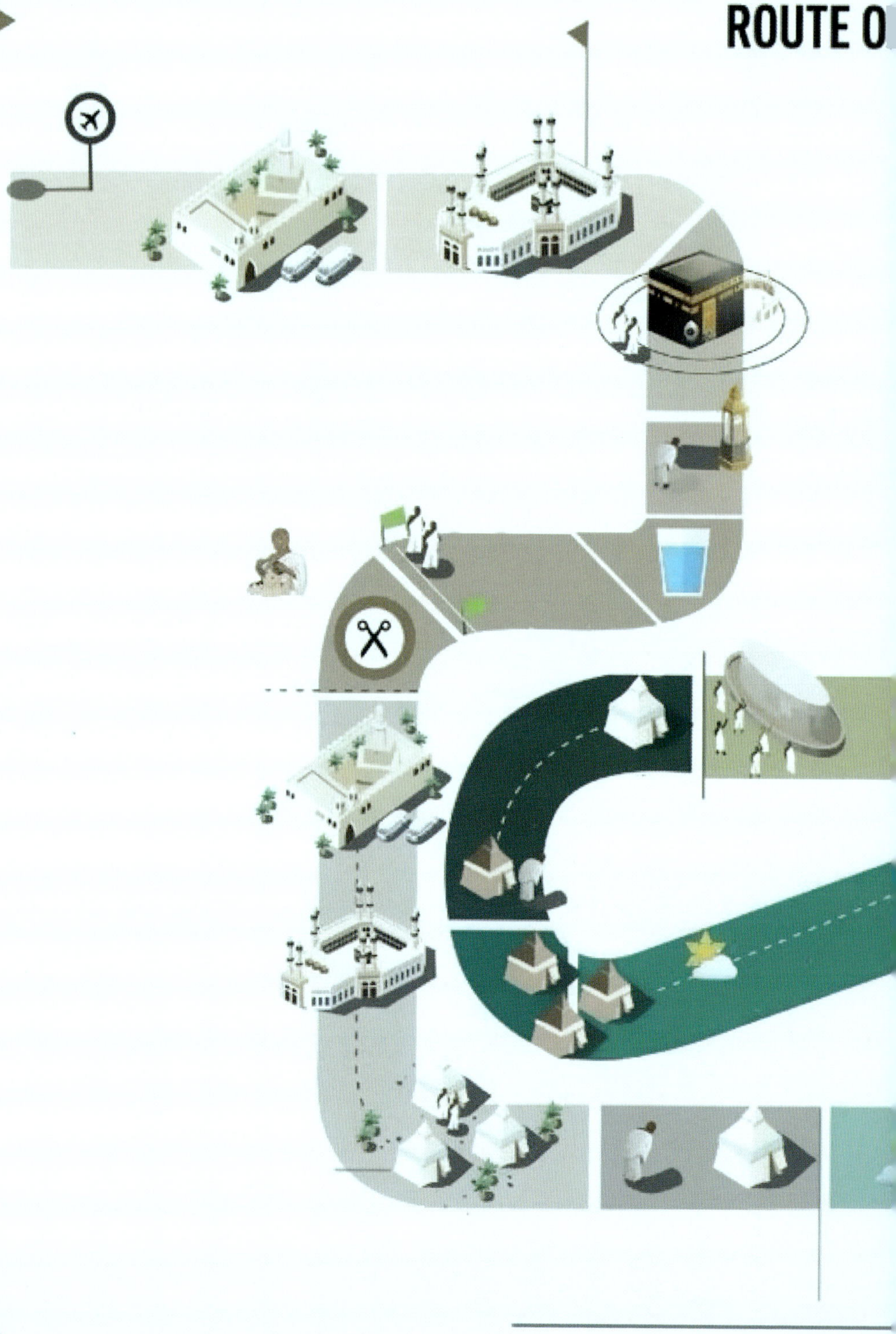

مناسك

AND UMRAH

Lesson 26

Salaf as-Salihin – Virtues and Stories

We must have love and respect for all of the Rightly Guided Caliphs and all of the Ahl al-Bayt (the Family of Prophet Muhammad ﷺ). We must never take sides with one against the other. Whoever sides with one against the other is cursed and has nothing to do with Islam or the Prophet of Allah ﷺ.

Every Muslim must respect the Companions, because they were the people who supported the Prophet ﷺ and gave their lives, wealth and time for the cause of Islam. In the same way, every Muslim must love the family and descendants of Prophet Muhammad ﷺ because of their blood relation to him ﷺ and because of our love for him ﷺ.

Respecting the Companions and loving the family and descendants of the Prophet ﷺ is a sign that our faith in Allah and love of the Prophet ﷺ are true. Whoever does not fulfil this important condition cannot be called a true Muslim, because such a person is closer to being a hypocrite than an honest believer in Allah and His Messenger ﷺ.

After the Prophet's family and Companions, we must respect the early Muslims who were the students and companions of the Prophet's family and Companions. The first three generations of Muslims have a special status in Islam because of their closeness to the Prophet ﷺ. The first three generations are known as '**as-Salaf as-Salihin**' (the Righteous Predecessors).

Each generation from the first three generations have been given the following terms:

1. The **Sahabah** (the Companions), the first generation of Muslims who met the Prophet ﷺ.
2. The **Tabi`in** (the Successors), the second generation of Muslims who met the **Sahabah**.
3. The **Tab` at-Tabi`in** (the Followers), the third generation of Muslims who came after and followed the Tabi`in.

The Prophet ﷺ praised the first three generations and declared them the best generation of Muslims. He ﷺ said, "The best of my Ummah is my generation, then the generation that follows it, then the generation that follows it." (al-Bukhari)

The great scholars and friends of Allah from the first three generations are our guides and shining examples to get closer to Allah and His Messenger ﷺ. They are the spiritual predecessors of the Muslim Ummah. The lives and accounts of some of the greatest people from the first three generations have been given below.

1. Uways al-Qarani

Uways bin `Amir was a great **Tabi`i (Successor)** who was from Yemen. He became a Muslim during the Prophet's lifetime, but he was not able to meet him because he used to take care of his mother.

It is reported that when people from Yemen came

to help the Muslim army, `Umar bin al-Khattab asked them, "Is there anyone called Uways bin `Amir among you?"

He continued searching until he met Uways and asked, "Are you Uways bin `Amir?"

"Yes," replied `Uways.

"Are you from the tribe of Qaran?" `Umar asked.

"Yes," replied Uways.

"Did you suffer from leprosy and then you were cured from it apart from the space of a dirham?" he asked.

"Yes," replied Uways.

"Is your mother still alive?" he asked.

"Yes," replied Uways.

Then `Umar continued, "I heard the Prophet of Allah ﷺ say: 'There will come to you Uways bin `Amir with the support from the people of the Yemen. He will be from Qaran, the branch of Murid. He had been suffering from leprosy from which he was cured but for a spot of a dirham. He looked after his mother in the best way. If he were to take an oath in the name of Allah, Allah would honour that. And if it is possible for you, then do ask him to beg forgiveness for you (from your Lord).'"

So, Uways prayed for him. `Umar then asked, "Where are you going?"

"To Kufa," replied Uways.

`Umar told him to wait and he wrote a letter to its governor, but Uways did not want him to write it saying, "I like to live among the poor."

The next year, a person from Kufa came to perform the Hajj. There he met the second Rightly Caliph, `Umar, who asked him about Uways al-Qarani. He then told the man about what the Prophet ﷺ said about him. When the man returned to Kufa he asked Uways al-Qarani to pray for him, but Uways refused and said, "You have just returned from the Pilgrimage. You should pray for me."

The man asked again but Uways gave the same reply. "Did you meet `Umar?" asked Uways.

"Yes," replied the man.

Uways then prayed for that man that Allah forgives him. After that incident, everyone in Kufa began to know of the spiritual status and the high rank of Uways al-Qarani. They all started going to him to ask him to pray for them. However, Uways did not like this newfound attention. He wanted to remain unknown to the people and spend his days and nights worshipping Allah. So, he left Kufa and did not return (Muslim).

Uways al-Qarani kept a simple lifestyle and he would pray all night. The scholars have said that he died during the battle of Siffin fighting on the side of the fourth Rightly Guided Caliph, `Ali bin Abi

Talib. Some of them have even said that the hadith, "Because of the intercession of a man from my Ummah, more people than the tribe of Banu Tamim will enter Paradise," (at-Tirmidhi) is regarding Uways al-Qarani, and that it shows his great status as one of the Friends of Allah.

2. Sa'id bin al-Musayyab

Sa`id bin Musayyab was a great **Tabi`i (Successor)**, who was born in Madinah in the year 15 AH, during the caliphate of `Umar bin al-Khattab. He was given the title '**`Alim Ahl al-Madinah**' (The Scholar of the People of Madinah) and **Sayyid at-Tabi`in** (the Master of the Successors). He used to narrate hadiths and was a scholar of fiqh (Islamic rulings). He was considered to be one of the seven jurists among the Tabi`in (Successors).

He studied with the great Companions of the Prophet ﷺ in Madinah. Among his teachers were: `Ali bin Abi Talib, `Uthman bin `Affan, `Abd Allah bin

`Abbas, `Abd Allah bin `Umar, Mother of the Believers `A'ishah, Zayd bin Thabit and Mother of the Believers Umm Salamah. He passed away in the year 95 AH and many of the great hadith scholars among the Salaf as-Salihin were from his students and they had received hadith through his chain of narration.

Imam ad-Darimi, the great hadith scholar, narrates that during the days of **Harra** (when Yazid sent his army to take over Madinah), the prayer was not held in the Prophet's Mosque for three days and there was no Adhan (Call to Prayer). Sa`id bin Musayyab took shelter in the Prophet's mosque and hid under the pulpit. During those three days, he would know the timing of the prayer because he used to hear some murmuring from the Prophet's grave and he used to know the prayer time had started (ad-Darimi).

3. Hasan al-Basri

Hasan bin al-Yasar was born in Madina in the year 21 AH and passed away in Basra, Iraq, in 110 AH. His mother was a servant of the Mother of the Believers Umm Salamah. He grew up among the blessed household of the Prophet ﷺ. Mother of the Believers Umm Salamah would give him milk to drink as a baby and take him to the gatherings of the Companions. It is reported that the second Rightly Guided Caliph, `Umar bin al-Khattab, prayed for Hasan al-Basri saying, "O Allah! Give him understanding of the religion and make him beloved to the people."

There is a famous incident regarding Imam Hasan al-Basri. The Imam had a neighbour called Shamoun, who was a fire-worshipper. Shamoun fell ill and was close to death. In fulfilling his neighbourly duty, Imam Hasan al-Basri decided to visit him and invite him to accept Islam. Shamoun was happy to accept his advice, but he said, "Three things hold me back from becoming a Muslim. The first is that you speak ill of the world, yet night and day you chase it. Secondly, you say that death is a fact to be faced, yet you make no preparation for it. And thirdly, you say that Allah will be seen in Paradise, yet today you do everything against seeking His pleasure."

"What you have said are not the words of those who reject Islam," Imam Hasan al-Basri replied. He explained that those Muslims who do not practice Islam will go to the Hellfire, but one day Allah will have mercy on them and take them out of it, but a person who rejects belief in Allah will not get this blessing of being freed from the Hellfire. He then said to the fire-worshipper, "Come now, you who have worshipped fire for seventy years; let us both put our hands into the fire, then you will see with your own eyes the weakness of fire and greatness of the power of God."

So, Imam Hasan al-Basri put his hand into the fire and held it there. Not a hair on his hand was burnt. When Shamoun saw this, he was amazed. "For seventy years I have worshipped fire," he said. "I am about to die. What am I to do?"

"Accept Islam," Imam Hasan al-Basri replied.

"If you give it to me in writing that Allah will not punish me," said Shamoun, "then I will believe, but until I have it in writing, I will not believe."

Imam Hasan al-Basri wrote it down. Shamoun wept, and he accepted Islam. He told Imam Hasan al-Basri of his final wish. He said, "When I die, instruct people to wash me, then bury me with your own hands, and place this document in my hand. This document will be my proof."

After he accepted Islam, Shamoun died shortly afterwards. That night Imam Hasan al-Basri went to sleep thinking about what he had done. "How can I promise someone protection from the Hellfire, when I do not have any protection for myself."

With this thought he fell asleep. He saw Shamoun in a dream. He had a crown on his head and was dressed nicely. Imam Hasan al-Basri asked him about his state, and he replied, "Allah has brought me here. He has showered upon me favours that are beyond all description. You have honoured your guarantee, so take your document. I do not need it anymore."

When Imam Hasan al-Basri woke up, he found himself holding the document in his hand. "Allah," he cried, "I know well that whatever You do does not need a reason. Who shall suffer loss at Your door? You granted a fire-worshipper of seventy years to come into Your presence because of a single word. How then will You exclude a believer of seventy years?" (Tadhkirat al-Awliya')

4. 'Umar bin `Abd al-'Aziz

`Umar bin `Abd al-`Aziz was a member of the Umayyad Dynasty, which ruled the Muslim world after the Rightly Guided Caliphs. He was born in 63 AH and died in 101 AH. Through his mother's side, he was a descendant of `Umar bin al-Khattab, the second Rightly Guided Caliph.

`Umar bin `Abd al-`Aziz is considered to be a reviver of the Islamic spirit at a time when there was much corruption and extravagance among the leaders. Through his sincerity and dedication, he brought the true teachings of Islam back into politics and made the leaders follow the rule of law. After the time of the Rightly Guided Caliphs, his rule is considered the best example of a true Islamic government.

There are many inspirational incidents to take from his life. Some of them, which are related to his simplicity and sincerity, are mentioned below.

Before `Umar bin `Abd al-`Aziz became the ruler of the Muslims, he owned a lot of wealth and land. When he was chosen to be the next ruler, he donated all of his personal belongings to the state and ordered his family and relatives to do the same. He adopted an extremely simple lifestyle to please Allah.

As the ruler of the Muslims, `Umar bin `Abd al-`Aziz was allowed to have endless privileges following in the tradition of the Muslim rulers at the time (the Umayyads) such as servants, slaves, maids, horses, palaces, golden robes and land but he rejected all of that and returned them to the state. For this reason, Malik bin Dinar said about him that people say I am a Zahid (someone who does not love the world) but in fact `Umar bin `Abd al-`Aziz is the Zahid because he was offered the world, but he rejected it.

His wish was to return to the way the Islamic government was during the time of the Rightly

Guided Caliphs. So, he led by example. He lived a very simple life. He did not live in a palace but a normal house with his wife.

One day, their servant went to his wife for food and she gave him chickpeas to eat. “Chickpeas? Every day?” he remarked. She smiled and replied, “Your Master, the Commander of the Faithful (Amir al-Mu’minin), eats it every day.” Such was the simplicity of his life and his disinterest in this world.

Once, while he was ill, people came to him to ask about him. His wife’s brother came into the room and noticed that the shirt `Umar bin `Abd al-`Aziz was wearing was dirty. He asked his sister to change it, but she said, “By Allah, he only has that one shirt.”

One day, `Umar bin `Abd al-`Aziz came home and asked his wife if she had a dirham (silver coin) so that he could buy grapes. She told him that they did not have any money. “You are the Commander of the Faithful (Amir al-Mu’minin), and you do not have a dirham to buy grapes?" she said. But `Umar bin `Abd al-`Aziz smiled and said, "Having wealth is worse for us than to be chained in the Hellfire." (Tarikh al-Khulafa' of as-Suyuti)

5. Rabi`ah al-`Adawiyyah

Rabi`ah al-`Adawiyyah is popularly known as Rabi`ah al-Basriyyah. She was born in Iraq towards the end of the first Islamic century and passed away in 180 AH. She was a famous Sufi Saint and one of the great female Friends of Allah (Awliya' Allah). She came from a poor family and had three older sisters. While she was a child, her father died, and she was raised as an orphan and then sent away to work as a house maid.

Despite the conditions she was born in, Rabi`ah was a blessed child. On the night of her birth, there was no oil in her house to light the lamp or any clothes for her to wear. Rabi`ah's mother asked her father to go next door and ask the neighbour for some oil, but he had made a promise not to beg anyone for anything. So, he went there and returned home and told his wife that he was not able to bring back anything for the child.

He was thinking about his situation with his head on his knees, when he fell asleep. He saw the Prophet ﷺ in a dream. He told him, "Do not be sad, for this daughter who is born is a great Saint and Friend of Allah who will intercede for seventy thousand people from my Ummah." The Prophet ﷺ told Rabi`ah's father to go to the governor of Basra and tell him that he says, "You send one hundred salutations upon me every night and four hundred every Friday night. However, this Friday you forgot to do so. So, as a penalty you must pay this person four hundred gold coins."

The father woke up and wrote a letter to the governor of Basra and sent it to him. The governor was overjoyed to receive this message and donated one thousand gold coins to the poor in gratitude to Allah that the Prophet ﷺ mentioned him. The governor went to meet Rabi`ah's father personally and gave him four hundred gold coins. He was honoured to meet the person who gave him the Prophet's message. He told her father to never hesitate in contacting him again if he needed anything. Then the father took the money and spent it on his daughter and on other needs the family had (Tadhkirat al-Awliya').

Lesson 27

The Four Imams

Among the Salaf as-Salihin (Pious Predecessors), there are four Imams who are of great significance. This is because they were the founders of the four schools of Islamic Law (fiqh). The vast majority of Muslims today follow one of these four **schools (madhhab)**. This is why it is important to learn about them. It has been the practice of the great scholars of Islam, from the time of the Salaf as-Salihin (Pious Predecessors) till today, to follow one of the four Imams.

Following one of these four schools is the best way to follow in the footsteps of the Salaf as-Salihin (Pious Predecessors). These four Imams were the greatest scholars of their generation — a generation whose excellence and virtue the Prophet ﷺ told us about. Their students and the many scholars who came after them developed their schools further and made them easy for us to study them today.

A brief description of the four Imams have been given below.

1. Imam Abu Hanifah

Nu`man bin Thabit is the founder of the **Hanafi School of Islamic Law (Madhhab)**. He is popularly known as Abu Hanifah. He was born in 80 AH in Iraq and passed away in 150 AH. He is the only Imam from the four Imams who met a Companion of the Prophet ﷺ. He is among the Tabi`in (the Successors), the second generation of Muslims. It is reported that he met the following seven Companions in his childhood:

1. Anas bin Malik
2. `Abd Allah bin Unays
3. `Abd Allah bin Juz'
4. Jabir bin `Abd Allah
5. Ma`qal bin Yasar
6. Wathilah bin al-Asqa`

7. `A'ishah bint `Ajrad

He is considered as one of the greatest scholars of Islam and was therefore given the title of '**al-Imam al-A`zam**' (The Greatest Imam). Many of the greatest scholars among the Salaf as-Salihin (Righteous Predecessors) were either his students or students of his students.

Among his popular students were Imam Abu Yusuf Ya`qub bin Ibrahim, who served as the chief judge during the rule of Harun ar-Rashid. He (Abu Yusuf) was the teacher of the fourth Imam, Imam Ahmad bin Hanbal. The other popular student of Imam Abu Hanifah was Imam Muhammad bin al-Hasan ash-Shaybani, who was the teacher of the third Imam, Imam ash-Shafi`i.

Imam Abu Hanifah was not an Arab. It is reported that the Prophet ﷺ foretold the appearance of Imam Abu Hanifah and mentioned his greatness in Islamic scholarship. Abu Hurayrah reports that the Prophet ﷺ said, "If the religion were among the stars, even then a person from Persia would have taken hold of it." In another narration, it states: "Even then a person among the children of the Persians would have taken hold of it." (Muslim)

Isma`il bin Hammad, the grandson of Imam Abu Hanifah, believed that the blessings his grandfather was given were the result of the prayer made for him by the fourth Rightly Guided Caliph, `Ali bin Abi Talib.

It is reported that Imam Abu Hanifah's grandfather was a convert to Islam. Once, during the celebration of Nayrouz (a Persian festival celebrating the new year), Imam Abu Hanifah's grandfather gifted `Ali bin Abi Talib a sweet dish, and `Ali bin Abi Talib in turn prayed for his son Thabit (Imam Abu Hanifah's father), saying, "May Allah bless him and his children." (Khatib al-Baghdadi)

Imam Abu Hanifah loved and respected the Prophet ﷺ very much. He would always honour his hadiths and follow them to the best of his ability.

His love for the Prophet ﷺ also extended to his family (the Ahl al-Bayt). He studied under Imam Muhammad al-Baqir, who was the grandson of Imam al-Husayn.

Imam ash-Shafi`i, who is one of the four Imams, would visit the grave of Imam Abu Hanifah. Whenever he would have difficulty in understanding some point of law, he would pray beside the grave of Imam Abu Hanifah and ask Allah for help through his blessings.

Imam al-Khatib al-Baghdadi records the words of Imam ash-Shafi'i, who said, "Certainly, I seek blessings by the means of Abu Hanifah and visit his grave daily. Whenever I have a need I perform two cycles of prayer and come to his grave and stand beside it, and I then ask Allah to fulfil my need. I do not go far except that my need is fulfilled." (Tarikh Baghdad)

Such was the love and respect between the Imams. Imam ash-Shafi`i recognised the great status of Imam Abu Hanifah and used to adopt his means to receive blessings from Allah, even though he had passed away.

2. Imam Malik

Malik bin Anas was born in Madinah in the year 93 AH and passed way in 179 AH. He is buried in Jannat al-Baqi. He is the founder of the **Maliki School of Islamic Law (Madhhab)** and he was one of the greatest among the Tab` at-Tabi`in (Followers), the third generation of Muslims. He studied under many great Tabi`in (Successors), among them were Nafi`, the freed slave of Ibn `Umar, and Ibn Shihab az-Zuhri.

He was considered to be one of the greatest scholars of his generation. Imam ash-Shafi`i used to say about him, "When the scholars are mentioned, Imam Malik is like a star. And Malik is Allah's proof for creation after the generation of the Tabi`in (Successors)."

He used to teach in the Prophet's Mosque all day, teaching people the hadith of the Prophet ﷺ. He only started teaching when seventy senior scholars recognised his scholarship.

Imam Malik compiled a hadith collection called '**al-Muwatta**'', and it is seen as one of the most authentic books after the Qur'an. He was known for his great respect and reverence for the hadith of the Prophet ﷺ. It is reported that whenever the Prophet ﷺ would be mentioned in front of Imam Malik, he would cry so much that the people around him felt sorry him. Out of his love for the Prophet ﷺ, he would not leave Madinah except to perform the Pilgrimage. (ash-Shifa of Qadi `Iyad)

Mus`ab bin `Abd Allah reports that whenever the Prophet ﷺ was mentioned Imam Malik's colour would change and he would bow his head until it would be difficult for the people around him to see him. Someone once criticised the Imam for this practice, but he replied, "You would not criticise me had you seen what I saw."

Once, the Caliph Abu Ja`far Mansur came to meet Imam Malik in the Prophet's Mosque. The caliph spoke loudly, and Imam Malik warned him, saying, "O Caliph! Do not raise your voice in the mosque of the Prophet ﷺ. Allah says in the Qur'an: '*O believers! Do not raise your voices above the voice of the Prophet.*'" (al-Hujurat 49:2) (ash-Shifa of Qadi `Iyad)

The Caliph Abu Ja`far al-Mansur asked Imam Malik, "Should I face the Qiblah while making the du`a or should I face the Messenger of Allah?" Imam Malik told him to face the grave of the Prophet ﷺ. He said, "Why would you turn your face away from the Prophet ﷺ when he is your means to Allah and your father Adam's means to Allah on the Day of Judgement? Rather, face him and seek intercession through his means so that he may intercede for you. Allah said, '*And, (O Beloved Prophet,) if they, having wronged their souls, had come to you imploring the forgiveness of Allah, and the Messenger had also asked forgiveness for them, then (owing to this means and intercession) they would certainly have found Allah Most Relenting,*

Ever-Merciful.'" (an-Nisa' 4:64) (ash-Shifa of Qadi `Iyad)

3. Imam ash-Shafi`i

Muhammad bin Idris is the founder of the **Shafi`i School of Islamic Law (Madhhab)**. He was born in 150 AH in Palestine, and passed away in 204 AH in Egypt. He was a famous student of Imam Malik and he also studied under Imam Muhammad bin Hasan ash-Shaybani, the student of Imam Abu Hanifah.

Imam ash-Shafi`i was an orphan. He memorised the Qur'an when he was seven years old and he memorised the Muwatta' (a hadith book compiled by Imam Malik) by the age of ten. When he was fifteen years old, he was a mufti (someone who is qualified to give legal rulings).

Imam ash-Shafi`i was known for his love for the Prophet ﷺ. He spent his life defending the Prophet's Sunnah. Muhammad bin Hasan al-Balkhi reports that he asked the Prophet ﷺ in a dream,

"O Messenger of Allah, what do you say about the opinions of Imam Abu Hanifah, Imam Malik and Imam ash-Shafi`i?" The Prophet ﷺ replied, "There is no opinion except my opinion. However, Imam ash-Shafi`i's positions are against the people of innovation (the people who do not follow the Sunnah)." (Siyar A`lam an-Nubala' of Imam adh-Dhahabi)

Ahmad bin Hasan mentions that he saw the Prophet ﷺ in a dream and he asked him about the differences between the scholars. He mentions that the Prophet ﷺ praised Imam ash-Shafi`i and said, 'He has revived my Sunnah.'

Imam ash-Shafi`i used to defend and protect the Sunnah of the Prophet ﷺ. Qutaybah bin Sa`id said, "When Imam ash-Shafi`i died, the Sunnah died with him. Imam Ahmad bin Hanbal will die, and then the deviations will come again." (Siyar A`lam an-Nubala' of Imam adh-Dhahabi)

Imam ash-Shafi`i used to express his love for the

Ahl al-Bayt (the Prophet's family). He once wrote a poem in which he prayed for their intercession on the Day of Judgement. Imam ash-Shafi`i writes:

> The Ahl al-Bayt are my medium and they
> are my means
> Through them I hope tomorrow to be given
> my book in my right hand
>
> (as-Sawa'iq al-Muhriqah of al-Haytami)

Imam ash-Shafi`i was a great and blessed scholar. Imam Ahmad bin Hanbal used to pray to Allah through his means. Once, his son `Abd Allah bin Ahmad asked his father about this, and he said, "Indeed, ash-Shafi`i is like the sun for humankind and like comfort for the body." (an-Nabhani in Shawahid al-Haqq)

4. Imam Ahmad bin Hanbal

Ahmad bin Muhammad bin Hanbal was the founder of the **Hanbali School of Islamic Law (Madhhab)**. He was from an Arab family and was born in Baghdad in the year 164 AH. He passed away in 241 AH. He studied under Qadi Abu Yusuf, the senior student of Imam Abu Hanifah. He had more than 280 hadith teachers, many of whom were great authorities among the Salaf as-Salihin (Pious Predecessors).

Imam Ahmad is considered one of the greatest hadith scholars. He compiled the 'Musnad', which contains more than 27,000 hadiths. This hadith compilation is among the largest collection of hadith compiled by any hadith scholar. He was also the teacher of many of the great hadith compilers. Among his prominent students were Imam al-Bukhari, Imam Muslim, Imam Abu Dawud and Imam Ibn Majah, among others.

He also met many of the great Friends of Allah (Awliya' Allah) and the Sufi Shaykhs from the Salaf as-Salihin (Pious Predecessors). During his lifetime, he met Dhu an-Nun al-Misri, Bishr al-Hafi, Ma`ruf al-Karkhi and as-Sirri as-Saqati.

Imam Ahmad bin Hanbal was very humble and modest when he was with the Sufis. If anyone asked him about the laws of Islam, he would give them an answer and explain it in detail. If the question was related to the spiritual realities, he would send them to Bishr al-Hafi, and tell the questioner to ask him because Bishr al-Hafi knew the spiritual realities better than him (Tadhkirat al-Awliya' of Imam Farid ad-Din `Attar).

Imam Ahmad bin Hanbal was a spiritual person who used to believe in the practice of taking blessings from the Prophet's hair. His son, `Abd Allah bin Ahmad, narrates that he saw his father taking the hair of the Prophet ﷺ and kiss it. He believed his father used to take the Prophet's hair and put it on his eyes and put it in water, after which he would drink the water to seek cure from illness (Siyar A`lam an-Nubala' of Imam adh-Dhahabi).

He was also a great protector of the Sunnah of the Prophet ﷺ. When the Mu`tazilah took control of Baghdad, they started oppressing the Sunni scholars to accept their beliefs. Imam Ahmad bin Hanbal did not back down from the Sunnah and he stood firmly by the truth. So, the Mu`tazilah arrested Imam Ahmad bin Hanbal and tied both his hands to a pole. He did not have anything to wear except a loin cloth.

The Mu`tazilah whipped him over one hundred times, but Imam Ahmad bin Hanbal did not give in and stood by the truth. As the persecution was continuing, his loin cloth became loose and his nakedness was about to show. Miraculously two hands appeared, and they tied his loin cloth tightly making sure that it did not fall. When the people saw this miracle, they became agitated, and wanted Imam Ahmad to be freed from the torture (Tadhkirat al-Awliya' of Imam Farid ad-Din `Attar).

Allah honoured Imam Ahmad bin Hanbal even after he passed away. Imam Ibn al-Jawzi mentions that the chief judge `Ali bin al-Husayn az-Zaynabi mentioned to him that a fire broke out in the chief judge's house. He said that all his books got burnt, except for the books hand written by Imam Ahmad bin Hanbal.

In another report, there was a flood in Baghdad and the graveyard in which Imam Ahmad bin Hanbal was buried in was also flooded. But his grave was protected because the water would not reach his grave as though there was a protective wall around it (Siyar A`lam an-Nubala' of Imam adh-Dhahabi).

Similarly, the daughter of Imam Ahmad bin Hanbal mentioned the incident relating to her brother, Salih. She reports that as the house was under fire, her brother said that it does not worry him that he had lost his house in the fire, but he was upset that his father's shirt was in the house.

He said he used to pray whilst wearing the shirt, which belonged to his father and he used to seek blessings through it. She said as the fire was put out, they entered the home and found that everything was burnt. But Imam Ahmad bin Hanbal's shirt was lying there on the bed. It was safe while everything around it was burnt and damaged (Siyar A`lam an-Nubala' of Imam adh-Dhahabi).

Lesson 28

The Awliya` Allah (Part 1)

The greatest people among humankind are the Prophets and Messengers. They have a special status with Allah because they are Allah's representatives to humanity. Other than the Prophets and Messengers, there are some who are neither Prophets or Messengers, but they have a special status with Allah. These special people are known as the '**Awliya' Allah**' (the Friends of Allah).

When Allah loves someone, and that person becomes His friend, that person is known as a '**Wali**' (a Saint). A Wali (Saint) is a person who always worships Allah sincerely and does not do any good deed for any worldly benefit. He only cares about serving Allah and helping His creation. Due to this sincerity and good intentions, Allah will make the Wali (Saint) an intercessor on the Day of Judgement to help those in need.

`Umar bin al-Khattab relates that the Prophet ﷺ said, "There are people from the servants of Allah who are neither Prophets nor Martyrs; the Prophets and Martyrs will envy them on the Day of Resurrection."

The Companions asked, "O Messenger of Allah! Tell us, who are they?"

He replied, "They are people who love one another for the sake of Allah, without having any shared family relations and giving wealth to one another. By Allah, their faces will glow with light and they will be sitting on pulpits of light. They will not fear anything (on the Day of Judgement) when people will fear, and they will not grieve when the people will grieve. He then recited the verse: *'Beware! Verily, the friends of Allah (Awliya' Allah) will not have any fear, nor will they grieve.'"* (Abu Dawud and an-Nisa'i)

From this hadith we can see the great status of the Awliya' Allah. All of the personalities among the Salaf as-Salihin (Pious Predecessors) that have been mentioned earlier were also the greatest Awliya' Allah. Details about other well-known Awliya' Allah (Saints) have been given below.

1. Sufyan ath-Thawri

Sufyan bin Sa`id ath-Thawri was born in 97 AH in Iraq and died in 161 AH. As well as being a great **Sufi** (someone who possesses the inward knowledge of the religion), he was one of the great Imams of Fiqh (Islamic Law) and Hadith. He was given the title of 'Commander of the Faithful' (Amir al-Mu`minin) because he was a great leader among the Muslims, teaching them the Sunnah of the Prophet ﷺ. Even though his knowledge in Fiqh (Islamic Law) and Hadith was great, he was better known as a Sufi.

The following story teaches us about who a Sufi is. Imam Ibn al-Jawzi writes about the Sufi's behaviour in Silwat al-Ahzan. He writes that their Imam, Shaykh Sufyan ath-Thawri, was taking a bath in the Tigris River one Friday. He took off his clothes and left them on the bank of the river. Suddenly, a thief appeared and stole the clothes.

Worried that his clothes were taken, Sufyan ath-Thawri sat there. The thief, however, returned with his clothes in his hand. He returned the clothes to the Shaykh and begged him to pray for the recovery of his right hand, which had become paralysed.

When Sufyan ath-Thawri took back his clothes, he did not say anything. He asked, "What happened to your hand?"

"It has become paralysed," the thief replied, and Allah knows best how long it was in that state.

Sufyan ath-Thawri raised his hands in prayer and said, "O Allah! In the way that You returned my clothes to me, so return to him the use of his hand."

Sufyan ath-Thawri was not concerned about the difficulty the thief placed him in, when he stole his clothes, but he was concerned about his wellbeing and happiness. This is the manner of behaviour which the Sufis, the Friends of Allah (Awliya' Allah), adopt when they deal with people. A Sufi does not care about himself as much as he cares about other people. Following this behaviour is the true path to Allah and it is the best way of becoming Allah's friend (Wali).

2. Ibrahim bin Adham

Ibrahim bin Adham al-Balkhi was born in Afghanistan around the year 100 AH and passed away in 165 AH. He was a great Sufi Shaykh, who was from the third generation of Muslims, the Tab` at-Tabi`in (Followers). He learnt hadith from Muhammad bin Ziyad, who was the companion of the famous Companion Abu Hurayrah. Among his teachers were the great hadith scholar Malik bin Dinar and the Imam of the Ahl al-Bayt, Imam Muhammad al-Baqir.

He was a prince, but he left the royal palace to become a Sufi. It is reported that he was sleeping one night, when he heard footsteps on the roof of his palace. He went out to see who it was, and he saw a man walking on the roof. He asked the man what he was doing, and the man replied that he was looking for his camel. Amazed at what he heard, Ibrahim bin Adham said, “Ignorant fool! Do you look for your camel on the roof?”

The man smiled at Ibrahim bin Adham and said, “Do you think you can find Allah while living in the palace?”

This question astonished Ibrahim bin Adham and it brought a change in his heart. He made the decision to leave the palace at once and to turn his back to the world and become a Sufi. For the rest of his life, he spent his days and nights worshipping Allah and not seeking the fame and fortunes of the world.

The following story shows the behaviour of the Sufis and the Friends of Allah (Awliya’ Allah) as shown by the Sufi Ibrahim bin Adham.

It is reported that Ibrahim bin Adham was once walking when he was confronted by a drunk young man riding a horse. The drunk man lashed out at Ibrahim bin Adham with his whip and ordered him to pick up his bottle of wine. Ibrahim bin Adham did this and he went with the young man to his house. There, in the house, was a musician who was playing a musical instrument. When Ibrahim bin Adham put the bottle of wine down, the drunk man took the musician's tambourine and hit Ibrahim bin Adham's head with a lot of force. Not only did he hurt Ibrahim bin Adham's head, but the tambourine also broke.

Ibrahim bin Adham left and went to the Tigris River to wash himself and his blood-stained clothes. He had no fear that his head was hurt, but he was upset that because of him the musician's tambourine had been damaged. When he returned home, he could not find anything, except a prayer rug. He took his prayer rug to the market and sold it.

He then returned to the drunk young man's house and gave half the money he made from the prayer rug to him as a gift and said, "When you hit the tambourine on my head, I'm sure you must have hurt your hand. So please accept this as a gift." Seeing his good gesture, the youth fell to the Sufi's feet and sincerely asked for forgiveness for his misbehaviour.

Ibrahim bin Adham then went to the home of the musician and gave him the rest of the money. He told him that the tambourine had been damaged because of his head, and so he is giving him this money to make up for the damage. The musician, seeing the excellence of his behaviour, fell to the Sufi's feet and sincerely repented to Allah from his sinful life.

3. Fudayl bin `Iyad

Fudayl bin `Iyad was born in the year 107 AH and passed away 187 AH. He is better known as an Imam among the Sufis, but he was also a great hadith scholar. He learnt hadith from the great scholars of hadith such as al-A`mash and he also studied under one of the great Imams of the Ahl al-Bayt, Imam Ja`far as-Sadiq. He was one of the great scholars of the Salaf as-Salihin (Pious Predecessors) who brought together both the outward and inward religious knowledge.

There are several stories about his repentance. In his youth, Fudayl bin `Iyad was a well-known thief. People used to fear travelling at night because of him. He used to rob people, but he also used to write the names of the people and what he had stolen from them. It is reported that one day he was carrying about his normal business when he heard someone reciting the following verse of the Qur'an: "*Has the time not (yet) come for the believers that their hearts get humbled with tenderness for the remembrance of Allah.*" (al-Hadid 57:16)

As soon as he heard this verse, it pierced his heart like an arrow. He sighed to himself in regret and said, "How long will I continue on this path of treachery. Now the time has come that I tread the path of Allah." After that he cried continually and then started his life afresh in the worship and obedience of Allah.

It is also said that while he was about to rob some travellers one day, he heard one of the travellers reciting the following verse of the Holy Quran: "*Say: 'O servants of Mine who have sinned, do not lose hope of Allah's mercy. Assuredly, Allah forgives all sins (and excesses). He is certainly Most Forgiving, Ever-Merciful.*" (az-Zumar 39:53)

When he heard this verse, it changed the direction of his heart. A wish was created in him to get closer to Allah. He went to the reciter who knew the Qur'an by heart and asked him, "Will Allah also forgive a thief and one who does major sins like me?" The man replied that if a person is at the door of repentance, it is open for him. Allah has promised that whoever comes to him and sincerely repents is surely forgiven. Then Fudayl bin `Iyad repented at the hand of that reciter.

After that he went to all the people who he had robbed, because he had written their names down, and he returned their property to them. They were happy to receive their stolen goods back. One Jewish man, however, was not happy with his money being returned. He said that he read in the Torah that if a follower of Prophet Muhammad ﷺ who has repented was to strike dust with his hand, it would turn into gold. He filled a pot with pebbles and asked Fudayl bin `Iyad to touch it. He touched it and the pebbles turned to gold.

4. Ma`ruf al-Karkhi

Ma`ruf bin Fayruz al-Karkhi was born around 132 AH, in Iraq, and died around 200 AH. He was born into a Christian family. His parents sent him to a Christian teacher as a child, and the teacher told him to say that God is one of three. But Ma`ruf al-Karkhi refused and said, "God is One!" His teacher beat him, and Ma`ruf al-Karkhi ran away.

His parents got worried and wanted to find him. They said, "Which religion has he converted to so that we may follow the same religion as him." When he returned home, he told his family that he had become a Muslim, and they also accepted Islam and became Muslims with him.

Ma`ruf al-Karkhi was known for his piety and love for Allah. He was beloved to Allah and to the people. It is reported by his nephew that on a hot day, the people came to him to ask him to pray to Allah for rain. So, when they gathered to make the prayer for rain, Ma`ruf al-Karkhi did not even raise his hands for the prayer and it started to rain.

Such were the blessings of Ma`ruf al-Karkhi that anyone who prayed beside his grave would find their prayers answered. Ibrahim al-Harbi said, "The grave of Ma`ruf al-Karkhi is a tried and true remedy." Imam adh-Dhahabi explains that his grave is a blessed place where supplications are accepted like the way the supplications are accepted in the mosques (Siyar A`lam an-Nubala').

Ma`ruf al-Karkhi was a great Sufi and Wali from the time of the Salaf as-Salihin (Pious Predecessors). He was senior to Imam Ahmad bin Hanbal. On one occasion, some of the students mentioned Ma`ruf al-Karkhi to Imam Ahmad bin Hanbal saying that he does not have much knowledge of Fiqh (Islamic Law). Imam Ahmad told his students off for saying this. He said, "Hold your tongues! Is not knowledge except what Ma`ruf al-Karkhi has achieved?" What he meant by this is that achieving Allah's love and being near to Him is the real essence of knowledge.

Abu Bakr al-Hilmi narrates: We were with Shaykh Ma`ruf al-Karkhi sitting on the banks of the River Tigris, when suddenly a group of disruptive youths were singing loudly, dancing and drinking alcohol. The followers of Shaykh Ma`ruf al-Karkhi got angry by seeing this. "O Ma`ruf al-Karkhi, curse these youths," pleaded the followers, "because they were drinking, singing and dancing in your presence, and little respect did they show. Raise your hands in supplication against them."

Ma`ruf al-Karkhi raised his hands in supplication and prayed, "O my Lord! I ask you that you keep them happy in the life hereafter, as you have kept them happy in this life."

The followers calmed down and were no longer angry. "Master! We asked you to pray against them, so that they may be destroyed, instead you prayed for them," they complained.

With a smile on his face, Ma`ruf al-Karkhi replied, "I prayed that they remain happy in the life hereafter, as they are in this life. And if Allah decides to keep them happy in the life hereafter, then surely, He will give them the blessing of repentance, and they will certainly repent."

Such was the nature of the Sufis and the Friends of Allah (Awliya' Allah). Their only concern is for the happiness of others and saving people from the Hellfire. A true Saint only thinks about people's forgiveness and their connection with Allah. He never talks about destruction and causing others harm.

It was the day of Eid, and everyone was excited. Men, women and children were wearing their best clothes. They were meeting one another and greeting each other. However, the face of one of the children was down, and he looked sad.

Shaykh Sirri as-Saqati narrates that he saw Shaykh Ma`ruf al-Karkhi picking dates on this day of celebration. He asked him why he was doing this, and he replied, "The orphan child is upset because the other children have nice clothes to wear, and he has nothing to wear. I want to see this child happy too, so I am picking these dates and selling them so that I can buy him new clothes."

Shaykh Sirri as-Saqati protested and said that he could do it instead. And so, Shaykh Sirri as-Saqati took the child home and gave him new clothes to wear. He said, "The reward that I received on that day in the form of divine light has changed my inner state forever." (al-Fatuwwa of Imam as-Sulami)

Lesson 29

The Awliya` Allah (Part 2)

The Awliya' Allah (Saints) have a special status among the Ummah of the Prophet Muhammad ﷺ. Among the Salaf as-Salihin, many of them were Sufis. A **Sufi** is a person who loves Allah and does everything for His sake only. He is someone who takes the love of the world out of his heart and cares only about pleasing Allah.

Some hadiths on the virtue of the Awliya Allah have been related below.

Abu Hurayrah narrates that the Prophet ﷺ said, "Whoever has enmity with a friend (Wali) of mine, I declare war on him. A servant of mine does not get close to me by something more beloved to me than the thing I have made obligatory on him. My servant continues to get close to me through voluntary actions (Nafl) until I love him. When I love him, I become his hearing by which he hears; his sight by which he sees; and his hand by which he grasps and seizes; and his feet by which he walks. If he asks Me anything, I will certainly give it to him. If he asks Me for protection, I will certainly protect him." (al-Bukhari)

He also reports that the Prophet ﷺ said, "When Allah loves a person, Angel Jibra'il is called and he is told, 'Allah loves so-and-so, so you love him as well.' So Angel Jibra'il begins to love him, then Angel Jibra'il goes to the inhabitants of the Paradise and calls out to them, 'Allah loves so-and-so, so love him.' So, the inhabitants of the heaven begin to love that person and then acceptance is put into the hearts of the people for that person." (al-Bukhari and Muslim)

We will continue with the accounts and good morals of some of the great Sufis and Saints.

5. Bishr al-Hafi

Bishr al-Hafi was born in the year 179 AH and passed away in 227 AH. He learnt the way of the Sufis from

Fudayl bin `Iyad and followed the school of thought (madhhab) of Sufyan ath-Thawri. He lived in the same period as Imam Ahmad bin Hanbal.

Imam Ahmad bin Hanbal's students used to ask him why he would go to Bishr al-Hafi when he was the greatest Imam of his time. But Imam Ahmad bin Hanbal replied, "Yes, but Bishr al-Hafi is more knowledgeable than me about Allah." He used to go to Bishr al-Hafi and say, "Tell me about my Lord." (Tadhkirat al-Awliya' of Farid ad-Din Attar)

Before Bishr al-Hafi became a Sufi, he was walking one day on the street drunk. He found a piece of paper on the floor on which it was written, 'In the name of Allah, the Most Merciful, the Most Kind.' Bishr al-Hafi picked up that piece of paper and took it home with him. He cleaned it and perfumed it with roses and put it in a high place in his house to show respect to it.

That night, a pious man had a dream in which Allah told him to tell Bishr al-Hafi, "You have perfumed My name, so I will perfume you. You have exalted My name, so I will exalt you. You have purified My name, So I will purify you. By My Majesty, I will perfume your name in this world and the world to come."

The pious man who had the dream did not understand it because he knew Bishr was a drunk, but he decided to tell Bishr about the dream anyway. When Bishr received this message, he understood its meaning and he left his life of sin. He became a Sufi and turned his back to the world. For the rest of his life, he lived as a slave of Allah and did not give any concern to the pleasures of this world (Tahdkirat al-Awliya' of Farid ad-Din `Attar).

The Sufis always look after all of Allah's creatures. They do not think about themselves as much as they do for others. It has been reported about Bishr al-Hafi that on one intensely cold day, he took off his clothes and began shivering. His followers saw this, and they asked, "Abu Nasr, what is the matter?"

"I just remembered a poor person who had nothing, and I had nothing to give him," Bishr al-Hafi replied. "So, I wanted to show concern for that person and share in his sadness."

Bishr was known as 'al-Hafi' (the Barefooted). He would walk around the streets and alleyways of Baghdad without wearing any shoes. Out of respect for him, the animals would not drop their dung on the streets of Baghdad so that his feet would not become dirty. He never used to wear shoes because when he repented to Allah from his sinful life, he was barefooted, so he wanted to remain in that simple lifestyle for the rest of his life. He would say, "My Lord, Allah, guided me when I was barefooted, and I will remain like this till I die."

6. Ba-Yazid Bistami

Abu Yazid Tayfur bin `Isa bin Surushan was born in the year 188 AH and died in 261 AH. His grandfather was a Zoroastrian (fire worshipper) who converted to Islam. He was known for his many spiritual insights and experiences. In Siyar A`lam an-Nubala', Imam adh-Dhahabi referred to him as the 'Sultan of the Saints' (Sultan al-`Arifin). His father and grandfather studied under the great Imam of the Ahl al-Bayt, Imam Ja`far as-Sadiq.

Imam adh-Dhahabi reports that Ba-Yazid Bistami used to say, "I have not found anything more difficult than seeking knowledge and acting on it." The Imam also reports that someone said to Ba-Yazid in amazement that you can fly in the sky, but Ba-Yazid used to reply, "What is so great about that? This bird, which eats dead meat, can also fly in the sky." He used to tell his followers not to be astonished with people who perform miracle-like acts, because they may have no value before Allah. A person's real value is in him following Allah's commandments (Shari'ah) and the Prophet's Sunnah.

One day Ba-Yazid Bistami was passing by a graveyard when a drunk youth was playing the lute (a stringed instrument). Seeing this sinful act, he asked Allah for protection. The youth did not like this, and he took the lute and violently hit Ba-Yazid's head with it, which resulted in the lute breaking.

Ba-Yazid Bistami was upset by the lute breaking. He had no concern that his head was bleeding. He went home and sent back some money and sweets. He asked the drunk youth to buy himself a new lute and to enjoy the sweets so that the pain of losing the lute can be buried away.

The drunkard was left amazed by seeing how his evil act was repaid with good, and the excellent behaviour of the Sufi. He began to feel sorry for his behaviour, and with a heavy heart, he went to Ba-Yazid Bistami and asked him for forgiveness.

There is another story showing the Sufis' good manners and kind treatment to others. Ba-Yazid Bistami's neighbour was a Jew, and he had set out on a journey, leaving his wife and small child at home. His wife did not have much belongings to keep her house lit in the night with an oil-lamp, and because of the darkness, the child kept on crying all night. Hearing about this situation, Ba-Yazid Bistami decided to go to the local market and buy some oil for his neighbour.

When the neighbour returned home from his journey after some time, his wife explained the whole situation to him, and he became embarrassed. He went to Ba-Yazid Bistami and thanked him for his kindness, but Ba-Yazid simply replied, "It was the neighbour's right, and the right of the neighbour is great in the sight of Allah. I did not do you any favour, because this is what my religion commands me to do. Islam has emphasised the right of the neighbour and good treatment to them. I was simply trying to fulfil this right."

Surprised by this, the neighbour said, "If your religion teaches you to treat people of other religions with such kindness, then I accept this true and beautiful religion." He then took out his hand and asked to be brought into the religion of Islam. The Sufi Ba-Yazid Bistami may have brought oil to light the Jew's home, but the truth was he brought light to his heart and blessed him with faith forever.

7. Sayyidah Nafisah at-Tahirah

Nafisah bint Hasan was born in the year 145 AH in Makkah and passed away in 208 AH in Cairo, Egypt, where she is buried. She was a shining Saint who came from the Ahl al-Bayt. Her father, al-Hasan al-Anwar, was the son of Zayd al-Ablaj, who was the son of Imam al-Hasan bin `Ali, the grandson of the Prophet ﷺ.

When she was five years old, she moved to Madinah with her family. She studied hadith and fiqh in Madinah from many of the great scholars of her generation. Her father married her to a man from the Ahl al-Bayt; his name was Ishaq, and he was the son of Imam Ja`far as-Sadiq, who is the son of Imam Muhammad al-Baqir, the grandson of Imam al-Husayn.

She moved to Egypt with her husband Ishaq bin Ja`far as-Sadiq and lived in Cairo. Imam ash-Shafi`i would visit her regularly and ask her for her prayers and blessings.

She is known as 'Nafisah at-Tahirah', which means 'the Rare Lady of Purity'. She was a great scholar and had a lot of knowledge, but she was better known for her piety, saintliness and closeness to Allah. She performed Hajj thirty times on foot.

Even today, her grave is visited by many people from all over the world. Imam adh-Dhahabi writes that it has been reported that she was a pious and devout lady, and that prayers and supplications would be accepted beside her grave, like the way prayers are accepted by the graves of the Prophets (Siyar A`lam an-Nubala').

Sayyidah Nafisah was greatly loved by everyone and especially the Egyptians. She was a great source of blessings for them. Many miracles have been recognised to have happened because of her. A popular miracle is of a Jewish girl who recovered from her paralysis. It is reported that when Sayyidah Nafisah arrived in Egypt and settled in her home, there was a non-Muslim family living nearby whose daughter was paralysed from the waist down.

One day, the girl's mother brought her to Sayyidah Nafisah to look after while she went shopping. She left her daughter in one corner of Sayyidah Nafisah's house. Sayyidah Nafisah began making ablution and water from her ablution flowed towards the girl. As the water touched the body of the girl, she experienced something strange. She began to take the water from Sayyidah Nafisah's ablution and rub it on her paralysed feet and legs. Suddenly by Allah's mercy, the paralysis disappeared completely, and she could stand.

Meanwhile Sayyidah Nafisah was busy in prayer. The girl stood up and seeing her mother just returning from the market, ran to meet her to tell her what had happened. Her mother cried with joy and declared, "That woman is truly holy, and her religion is the truth." She came in, hugged Sayyidah Nafisah, thanked her for healing her daughter and asked her to pray that she can be guided from darkness to light. Sayyidah Nafisah then taught her to recite the Shahadah and they became Muslims.

When the father of the girl returned home that evening, he saw that his daughter was cured and he was overjoyed. He asked his wife what had happened, and she told him the whole story. He raised his head to the heavens and said, "O Allah! You guide whom You like, and I now know that Islam is the true religion, completing what we believe in."

He went to the home of Sayyidah Nafisah and said, "I believe in your religion, and I accept it. I testify that there is none to worship except Allah and that your grandfather Muhammad ﷺ is the

Prophet of Allah." That miracle was the cause for the entire tribe of Sayyidah Nafisah's neighbour to enter Islam (Imam Metawalli ash-Sha`rawi).

8. Shaykh `Abd al-Qadir al-Jilani

Shaykh `Abd al-Qadir al-Jilani is the greatest of the Awliya' Allah (Saints) after the time of the Salaf as-Salihin (Pious Predecessors). He was born in the year 470 AH in Gilan, an area of present-day Iran. He was a leading Imam from the Ahl al-Bayt, whose family line goes back to Imam al-Hasan. His father's name was Musa bin `Abd Allah.

Shaykh `Abd al-Qadir al-Jilani was the Shaykh al-Islam of his time. This title is only given to the greatest of scholars, who have learnt all of the religious sciences. He passed away in the year 561 AH and is buried in Baghdad. He is the founder of the **Qadiri Sufi Order (Tariqah)**, which has spread all over the Arab and non-Arab world and is one of the greatest Sufi orders in Islamic history.

He was the most authoritative Imam of the Hanbali School of Islamic Law (Madhhab) in his time. The great Hanbali jurist Ibn Qudama al-Maqdasi relates that he met Shaykh `Abd al-Qadir al-Jilani towards the end of the Shaykh's life. He said about him, "We stayed at his school and he used to take care of us. I believe he used to send his son Yahya to ask about us and light up the lamps for us. He used to send us food from his house and he would lead us in the prayers. During those days, no one used to read to him except us. We stayed with him for one month and ten days, then he passed away. We offered his funeral prayer in his school at night time. I have not heard anyone relate as many miracles performed by a person as the ones performed by him; and I have not seen anyone respected by a people more than him." (Siyar A`lam an-Nubala' of Imam adh-Dhahabi)

It is reported that 70,000 people used to attend his lectures regularly. The great warrior and Muslim ruler Salah ad-Din al-Ayyubi (Saladin) met Shaykh

`Abd al-Qadir al-Jilani when he was a child and took blessings form him and learnt from him. Later, when Salah ad-Din became the ruler of the Muslims, many of his soldiers were the students and disciples of Shaykh `Abd al-Qadir al-Jilani. This army of Sufis was blessed to free Jerusalem in 1187 CE from the Crusaders, who ruled over Palestine for almost a hundred years.

On one occasion, Shaykh `Abd al-Qadir al-Jilani set out to Makkah with the intention of performing the Hajj. When he reached a place near Baghdad, called Halla, he ordered his followers to find the most broken-down home, to spend the night there. He was offered to stay in the homes of the emirs and governors, but Shaykh `Abd al-Qadir al-Jilani refused their offer.

After much searching, they found a home in which an old man and woman, and a child were living. After seeking their permission, they stayed there that night. All the gifts they had received such as money and animals were gifted to them. Shaykh

`Abd al-Qadir al-Jilani also gave up his personal belongings and handed them over to the poor family. Through his kindness, he blessed them with such wealth the likes of which those around them had not received.

Shaykh `Abd al-Qadir al-Jilani once saw a poor person sitting in a corner alone, looking sad. He asked his followers to find out the cause of his suffering.

"I went to the bank of the river," explained the poor man, "and I did not have anything to give the sailor to ferry me across to the other side."

As soon as the poor man explained his situation, someone gifted Shaykh `Abd al-Qadir al-Jilani a bowl containing thirty coins. Shaykh `Abd al-Qadir al-Jilani gave the bowl to the poor man and told him to pay the sailor. Such was the Shaykh's kindness and generosity, and his care for others.

Lesson 30

Becoming Young Adults

As we get older, we become more responsible for our lives and actions. When we were babies, we did not have to go to school, or look after our younger brothers or sisters. We could play all day and not have to worry about anything, but as we got older, our parents sent us to school to learn to read and write. We became more responsible, and now we are expected to do our homework and to help our parents around in the house.

Learning to become responsible is an important part of growing up. As we grow up, our bodies keep on changing. When we were born, we did not have any teeth. So, our parents used to feed us. But then we grew teeth, and we started to eat on our own. We used to wear nappies, but then we grew bigger, and we stopped wearing nappies and started using the toilet on our own. We are changing every year, and one day we will become young adults.

Allah wants us to be responsible for our actions. So, He created special signs in our body to let us know that we have become young adults. Between the ages of 11 and 14, our bodies go through some very important changes. Some of these changes will make us feel different and may be uncomfortable, but we should not be worried because these bodily changes are all a part of growing up. When we start seeing these signs in our body, it means that we are not children anymore and that we are responsible for our actions.

The Signs of Maturity (Bulugh)

When a person becomes a young adult, we say that he is ‘**mature**’ (**Baligh**). Some of the signs that tell us that we have become ‘mature’ (Baligh) are the following:

- We become taller and our muscles get bigger. We may even put on more weight during this time. This is normal. When we pass this stage of our life, we lose this extra weight.
- We may experience sudden changes in our mood, or even other feelings such as low self-esteem, anxiety or depression.
- More hair grows on the body. Hair will grow in new places, such as under the armpits and around the private parts. For boys, they will start growing a moustache and beard. For girls, they may have some hair above their top lip. This is all normal and nothing to be worried about.

- Body odour becomes stronger because the body sweats more.
- We may develop acne (when spots appear on the face).
- Boys will experience a change in their voice, i.e., the voice breaks, and it becomes deeper.
- Boys will also experience a white sticky liquid coming out from their private part when they sleep. This is known as a 'wet dream' and the white sticky liquid is called 'semen'.
- Girls will experience bleeding from their private part. This is called 'menstruation' (or periods), and it happens every month and lasts for about one week.

When boys experience a wet-dream, or a girl experiences her periods, it means that they have become 'mature' (Baligh). Being mature (Baligh) means that you are now responsible for everything that you do. You have to perform all your prayers and make up any that you have missed, keep all the fasts in the month of Ramadan, start paying the Zakah if you have the Nisab (minimum amount) and perform the Hajj if you are able to. If you do not do any of these things, then you will be sinful, and you will be questioned by Allah on the Day of Judgement.

Ghusl (the Ritual Bath)

There are times when taking a bath or shower (Ghusl) becomes obligatory (Fard). As a general rule, whenever a man experiences a wet dream or releases semen (the white sticky fluid) from his body, it becomes **obligatory (Fard)** to perform the Ghusl (ritual bath).

In the same way, with women at the end of the menstruation (i.e. periods), the Ghusl becomes obligatory to be performed.

When we have a wet dream or release semen, we enter into a state of ritual impurity called '**Janabah**'. To come out of this impure state, the Ghusl must be performed. Make sure that every part of the body is washed with water and the mouth and nose are rinsed properly; otherwise you will still be in the impure state (Janabah). To come out of Janabah you must perform the Ghusl. Just doing the Wudu' on its own is not enough.

It is important to do the Ghusl (ritual bath) as soon as possible, because it is not good to remain in this state of impurity for long. While being in this state of Janabah (ritual impurity), it is **impermissible (Haram)** to recite the Qur'an or enter the mosque as well as not being able to pray the Salah, touch the Qur'an or perform the Tawaf. During the menstruation (periods), females cannot recite the Qur'an until the menstruation ends and the Ghusl (ritual bath) is performed.

Personal Hygiene

One of the most important responsibilities you will have as a young adult is to maintain personal hygiene. We should try to take a bath or shower at least 2-3 times a week.

As a 'mature' Muslim (Baligh), you must remove the extra hair growing under your armpits and around the private parts. This can be done by either shaving or trimming the hair. Hair removal cream can also be used. Boys need to trim their moustache regularly. Also, nails should be clipped regularly so they do not grow long.

Removing the hair from under the armpits and around the private parts, clipping the nails and trimming the moustache (for boys) are all natural practices of a normal human being. These natural practices are known as '**Fitrah**' and staying within the Fitrah is commanded by Allah. It is natural for males to grow a beard. Keeping a beard is from the Fitrah practices, and all the Prophets had one.

Prophet Muhammad ﷺ used to keep a beard and so this is also from his Sunnah (practice).

We should follow the above practices of personal hygiene on a regular basis. For example, we should clip the nails and trim the moustache on a weekly basis (preferably before the Friday Prayer) and remove the hair from under the armpits and around the private parts often such as every 15-20 days. If we leave it more than forty days, we will be sinful, as this is the maximum limit for these practices.

As Muslims, it is important to be well dressed and presentable. It is important to wear deodorant or perfume to remove the bad odours from our body, and to use toothpaste or mouthwash to keep away bad breath.

How we present ourselves influences the way people see us. If we are well kept and presentable, people will have a good impression of us.

Appendix

The Sirah Timeline

The Prophet's Age	Event
0 (570 CE)	Born in Mecca in the 'Year of the Elephants' on the 12th of Rabi` al-Awwal. His father `Abdullah died before he was born.
4 (574 CE)	He was looked after by his wet-nurse Lady Halimah al-Sa`diyyah and he went back to his mother at the age of 4.
6 (576 CE)	His mother Aminah died when he was 6. He was then looked after by his grandfather `Abdul Muttalib.
8 (578 CE)	His grandfather `Abdul Muttalib died when he was 8. He was then looked after by his uncle Abu Talib.
12 (582 CE)	Journey to Syria and meeting with Bahirah, the monk.
25 (595 CE)	The business trip to Syria and marriage to Lady Khadijah.
35 (605 CE)	Rebuilding of the Ka`bah and placing of the Black Stone in its corner.
38 (608 CE)	Signs of Prophethood start to appear more often.
39 (609 CE)	Staying in the cave of Hira' during Ramadan to worship Allah.
40 (610 CE)	The first revelation in the cave of Hira'.

Year of Prophethood	Event
Year 1 (610 CE)	The beginning of the Prophetic mission. Telling people about Islam secretly. Lady Khadijah, `Ali, Abu Bakr and Zayd bin Harithah follow Islam.
Year 3 (612 CE)	Telling people about Islam openly. The Prophet ﷺ invites his relatives to Islam.
Year 4 (613 CE)	The Quraysh attack the Muslims and begin to treat the Muslims badly.
Year 5 (614 CE)	Journey to Abyssinia.
Year 6 (615 CE)	Gathering in Dar al-Arqam to teach Islam secretly. Hamzah and `Umar follow Islam
Year 7 (616 CE)	The boycott and the retreat to the mountain pass of Abu Talib.
Year 10 (619 CE)	End of the boycott. The Year of Sorrow (Abu Talib and Lady Khadijah died in this year). Trip to Ta'if. The Night Journey and the Heavenly Journey.
Year 11 (620 CE)	The first meeting with the leaders from Yathrib.
Year 12 (621 CE)	The first pledge of al-`Aqabah
Year 13 (622 CE)	The second pledge of al-`Aqabah

Hijri Calendar	Event
1 AH (622 CE)	The journey to Madinah
	The building of Masjid an-Nabawi (Prophet's Mosque)
	The introduction of Adhan in the mosque
	The pact of brotherhood
	The pact of Madinah (state constitution)
2 AH (623 CE)	Change of the Qiblah from Jerusalem to Makkah
	Fasting in the month of Ramadan becomes part of Islam
	The amount of Zakat to pay is made clear and Sadaqat al-Fitr becomes part of Islam
	The Battle of Badr
	The first `Id prayer is offered
3 AH (624 CE)	The Battle of Uhud
	The drinking of wine is made Haram
	Wearing hijab for women becomes part of Islam
5 AH (626 CE)	The Battle of Khandaq (Trenches)

6 AH (627 CE)	The Muslims set out for `Umra
	The Treaty of Hudaybiyah
	Letters sent to different kings inviting them to Islam
	The Hajj becomes part of Islam
7 AH (628 CE)	The Conquest of Khaybar
	The Muslims do `Umrah
8 AH (629 CE)	The Conquest of Makkah
	The Battle of Hunayn
	The Battle of Ta`if
9 AH (630 CE)	The trip to Tabuk
	The Muslims do Hajj led by Abu Bakr
	The delegations to Arabic tribes
10 AH (631 CE)	The Farewell Pilgrimage
	The Farewell Sermon and the completion of the religion
11 AH (632 CE)	The Prophet ﷺ died at age of 63.

NOTES